HOME RUN

HOME RUN
A MODERN APPROACH TO BASEBALL SKILL BUILDING

MICHAEL McRAE

POLESTAR
BOOK PUBLISHERS

Polestar Book Publishers acknowledges the ongoing support of The Canada Council, the British Columbia Ministry of Small Business, Tourism and Culture, and the Department of Canadian Heritage.

All diagrams and illustrations by Jim Brennan
Cover design by Jim Brennan
Cover photograph by David Madison, reproduced with permission of
    Norman Owen Tomalin / Bruce Coleman Inc.
Printed and bound in Canada by Friesen Printers

CANADIAN CATALOGUING IN PUBLICATION DATA
McRae, Michael, 1969-
    Home run
    ISBN 1-896095-29-1
    I. Baseball–Training. I. Title.
GV875.6.M37 1998   796.3572   C97-910117-4

Library of Congress Card Catalog Number: 97-065828

POLESTAR BOOK PUBLISHERS
P.O. Box 5238, Station B
Victoria, British Columbia
Canada   V8R 6N4
http://mypage.direct.ca/p/polestar/

In the United States:
POLESTAR BOOK PUBLISHERS
P.O. Box 468
Custer, WA
USA   98240-0468

5 4 3 2 1

Acknowledgements

I would like to thank the following people for the help, support and wisdom they have offered me. Their assistance has been essential to my development in baseball and, to a larger degree, in life. My gratitude belongs to: Joe Bauth, Bill Byckowski, Wayne Burdon, Remo Cardinale, Mike Carnegie, Gene B. DeLorenzo, Dean DiCenzo, Larry Downes, John Gill, Rick Johnston, Darrel Kemp, Jeff Lounsbury, Murray Marshall, Jim Mauro, Judy and Al McRae (my parents), John Miller (my grandfather), Greg Minor, and the Toronto Blue Jays organization. Thank you.

To my wife, Michelle: Thank you for your support. Your remarkable strength is responsible for my pursuit of my dreams and ambitions. In fact, your urging made this ambition come true.

In loving memory of my mother, Judy Diane McRae.
I miss you, and with each passing day I notice more and more
of our similarities. May I continue to become more like you.

HOME RUN
A Modern Approach to Baseball Skill Building

FOREWORD

Acquiring excellent baseball skills does not happen by accident. It is the result of hard work, effort and quality technical instruction. In *Home Run: A Modern Approach to Baseball Skill Building*, Mike McRae provides the high quality instruction. The hard work and effort are the responsibility of coaches and players.

I was fortunate to play for thirteen years in Major League Baseball, so I can appreciate the time and effort it takes to improve skills and move to the next level of expertise. My own progress — like that of every player I know — did not come without solid instruction and advice along the way. I am certain that the concepts and drills presented by Coach McRae will provide similar benefits to those playing and teaching the game today.

It is a fact of baseball — and of life — that not every athlete is gifted with the ability of a Ken Griffey Jr. or the powerful arm of a Randy Johnson. The skills taught in the following pages will benefit players of all ages and levels of ability. Each chapter starts with the basics and then progresses to the development of higher level skills for the more advanced players. Furthermore, this book provides a thorough set of drills designed to improve players' abilities in all the different facets of the game. It offers players and coaches a sound base of instruction that will enable them to rise to the next level of competition.

Home Run reflects the knowledge and expertise of Coach McRae, who is one of college baseball's newest and more innovative instructors. McRae believes in building from a solid foundation, and in teaching his players sound fundamentals of the game. This coaching philosophy runs throughout the following pages, and is particularly evident in the amount of time and effort devoted to lower body mechanics — the key to building a solid base of skills. By employing the skills and drills described in *Home Run*, coaches and players can make practices effective, interesting and fun. The positive result: immediate improvement, increased confidence and greater enjoyment of the game.

Ernie Whitt
Toronto Blue Jays

"The harder you work, the harder it is to surrender."
— Marv Levy

INTRODUCTION

Home Run is an instructional baseball manual designed to offer coaches and players an effective, basic framework for learning the game. The skills and drills on these pages, if applied consistently, are guaranteed to produce good, solid ballplayers.

My goals are to offer a modern, dynamic approach to teaching and learning baseball skills. I encourage you to read my theories and methods with an open mind, try them, and then decide which method is best for you and your team.

I emphasize *muscle memory*, the body's solid platform on which all athletic skills are built. In order to condition their muscles to perform powerful, reliable movements, athletes must commit themselves to a consistent regimen of physical repetitions. Eventually, the muscles themselves will remember the most effective way to perform the targeted skill. It is vital that repetitions are practiced correctly from beginning to end. Unfortunately, bad habits can become muscle memory just as efficiently as good habits, so it is paramount that athletes maintain a consistent focus on accuracy of movement throughout.

I have been fortunate in receiving invaluable coaching tips from some professionals in the field. One of the most important lessons urged on coaches by Toronto Blue Jays instructors is, quite simply, *simplify*. Of course young players need to be instructed, guided and taught, which means the introduction of techniques and terms that define action. However, it would prove counter-productive to emphasize these at the expense of spontaneity, fluidity and ease. The object for coaches is to teach effective skills and strategies while emphasizing simplicity and avoiding confusion.

It would be an enormous instruction manual that defined each and every way a particular baseball skill could be performed. This is not that manual. Instead, *Home Run* directs its focus on basic methods for playing and teaching the game of baseball solidly and well. Consider this book a reliable guideline, and a foundation for the individual talents of aspiring coaches and players.

FIRST INNING

THROWING THE BASEBALL

THROWING THE BASEBALL

Throwing the ball is the first skill a player must master. Many coaches assume that every player will know how to throw a ball if they have played baseball. An attentive coach will observe the inevitable tossing around of the ball that takes place when players arrive at the park. A little observation of this preliminary workout often highlights areas where individual players need improvement. This will be the moment to plan how to turn weak arms into strong ones by paying attention to these areas, rather than hiding such players away in positions where no improvement is possible.

The throwing component of every practice and pregame warm-up must be monitored and directed. Rather than simply throwing the ball around, players need specific drills which are designed to improve their throwing mechanics. This warm-up is a vital opportunity for good coaches. If a player goes to the park three times a week and makes at least forty throws during each session, then he has participated in 120 repetitions that week. A 120-rep session is an extensive enough time period to develop habits — good and bad. Coaches have an excellent opportunity to promote good habits and a positive work ethic during these throwing sessions. In fact, the mere presence of an engaged, observing coach is likely to aid and ensure player concentration and focus.

I adhere to the theory that players "throw with their feet." The most important aspect of any skill area, from throwing to hitting to fielding, is the role of the lower body. So when teaching throwing mechanics, coaches should address the lower body first.

The complete throwing process involves the sequential movement of the body's parts. The back foot will square so that the instep faces the target. The glove-side foot will take a stride towards the target. Simultaneously, the hands will separate and the ball will complete an arc out of the glove, up and back in the opposite direction from the target. The shoulders will rotate and complete the arc as the arm and ball accelerate towards the target. Once the arm continues through to the front of the body, the wrist will snap straight down to release the baseball. The back leg will release from the ground as the arm continues forward.

SQUARE THE BACK FOOT

In preparing to throw the ball, square the back foot. If you are right-handed, take your right foot and turn it 90 degrees so that the instep is facing your target (the person receiving the ball) and the toes are pointing out and away from your left foot. If you are a left-handed thrower, then your left foot will turn so the instep is facing the target.

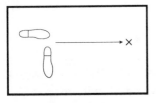

Square the back foot (RH).

Further develop this movement by taking a positive step when initiating this action. In other words, do not simply turn your back foot to square it up, but actually take a step towards your target when you square the back foot. This action helps you to develop momentum as you begin the throwing movement. Also, it will help to establish direction because the first step is directed at the target.

MAC FACT: *Take a positive step towards the target.*

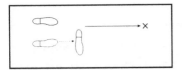

Take a positive step towards the target.

Learning at an early age to take a positive step and practicing it during throwing drills will prove helpful when learning other defensive skills. It is a common error to take a negative step (one that is neither straight nor covers significant distance) when making a throw after fielding a ground ball.

THE STRIDE

Once your back foot (right foot for right-handers) has been squared, then your other foot will take a normal walking stride towards the target. This action will occur naturally if you merely lift your other foot and let it fall. Because the back foot has begun to establish the direction, the other will fall into place and complete it.

Keep your weight on the balls of your feet. This weight distribution holds true for all skills in the game of baseball, as well as many others. Be sure not to land on the heel when taking your stride. Such landings put you at risk for injury and make balance problems more likely during throwing.

MAC FACT: *Avoid landing on your heel when taking your stride!*

At this time, both knees should be slightly flexed and the weight evenly distributed on both legs. Neither leg should be locked. Your head will be positioned between the centre of the body and the back leg.

When your feet are properly positioned, your entire body should have turned so that the left shoulder and left leg are facing the target, and the front of your body is positioned at a 90 degree angle to the target. For right-handers in this position, the left side of the body is now considered the directional side. The feet are

Stride and land on the ball of your lead foot.

responsible for establishing this correct direction. Hence the reason I believe that you "throw with your feet." Faulty direction at this phase of the throwing process decreases your chances of making a strong, accurate throw.

BREAK OF THE HANDS

As you set your feet, your hands should start together in the centre of the body, near the belly button. The belly button is a good starting point for the hands because it represents the centre of gravity on the body and helps to establish balance.

Break your hands with the thumbs pointing down.

Your hands will break from the belly button region with thumbs pointing down. The throwing arm will take the following route: out of the glove, down, back and up. The glove-side arm will follow a similar route in the opposite direction. The object is to raise your elbows to a point at least level with the shoulders. If you draw a line from the throwing elbow across the shoulders to the glove-side elbow, it should be straight and level. The elbows, shoulders and trunk of the body will form a solid "T" shape, establishing the correct "throwing position."

MAC FACT: *Break the hands with the thumbs pointing down.*

The positioning of the lower half of the glove arm (from elbow to finger tips) is not vital, as long as a straight line exists from elbow to elbow.

MAC FACT: *Elbow to elbow must be a straight line through the shoulders when the arm circle is completed.*

To complete the hand break action, you should be trying to create arc-like motions with your arms. The hand break will create two arcs similar to the letter "W." As age and skill level

Make an arm circle or an arc
to the Throwing Position.

The Throwing Position: the ball
must face the opposite direction.

increase, these circles will vary according to the positions being played. For example, catchers have a very short arm circle. They take the ball out of the glove straight to the back ear. Infielders' arms take a half-circle route. Outfielders and pitchers, however, want large circles when they break their hands.

THE "T" POSITION

The reason for breaking the thumbs down is to ensure that your fingers end up on top of the ball once you reach the "T" position. The goal of this throwing position is to have the ball facing away from your target. You want to get the ball to the "top of the hill" before you begin throwing.

The positioning of the fingers on top of the ball is crucial. If a player gets to the "T" position with the fingers underneath and the ball facing up to the sky, serious elbow damage may result. Furthermore, you cannot throw the ball as hard or as accurately with the fingers underneath. When coaches allow a bad habit such as this to continue, the player's health is in jeopardy. Remember the importance of the fingers being on top of the ball and the elbow at least level with or higher than the shoulder.

MAC FACT: *In the "T" position, the ball will be facing away from the target, fingers will be on top, and your throwing elbow at least at shoulder height.*

Again, the positioning of your lower arm is not important at this stage as long as your elbow-to-elbow line is achieved. Let comfort decide your glove position here.

THROWING ARM ACTION and ROTATION OF THE BODY

Once your elbows get the ball up to the "T" or throwing position, you are balanced and ready to throw the ball. Your trunk and hips will start the rotation of your body and encourage the acceleration of your arm.

Again, it is imperative that you keep your throwing elbow at least level with or higher than your shoulder in order to maintain better control and avoid injury. As the acceleration takes place, your arm, shoulder and wrist should be in a loose and relaxed state. In fact, slow-motion video will reveal that your elbow leads the acceleration so that it appears as if your lower arm (elbow to wrist) is actually parallel to the ground. Avoid tensing your arm during acceleration. Keep your shoulder controlled but relaxed. Your fingers must have a firm grip on the ball since, as your arm accelerates past your head, the ball has acquired enough force that it weighs around 50 pounds.

During the rotation of your body, your head and chest will lead your throwing arm towards the target. Hips must rotate in an aggressive manner. Your hips can increase the velocity of the ball while reducing the strain placed on your shoulder. Explode your hips while throwing by generating a quick, powerful rotation.

As you rotate, keep your elbow at or above shoulder height.

THE GLOVE SIDE

Since the body is symmetrical from left to right, your non-throwing, glove side is important for balance and control during the throwing motion.

Use your glove side to "sight your throw" – which is like looking down the length of an arrow before release – by using the straight line from your lead shoulder to your elbow.

"Sight the gun."

Pull the glove to your chest.

This line should be pointed at the target since your glove side is facing the direction of the throw. I teach players to pull their glove back to their chest as their throwing arm reaches their head. Another option is to tuck your glove in your armpit. This is dangerous for pitchers, though: if the ball is hit directly back at them, they don't have time to get the glove untucked.

MAC FACT: *As the ball is released, pull your glove back to your chest.*

If you lose concentration on your glove, it will probably drop to your side which results in tilting the head. When this happens your eyes are no longer level with the field, which hinders control by leaving you slow and disoriented.

Dropping your glove also affects throwing. When your head tilts, your throwing arm has a tendency to change release points. Usually, your arm will move further away from your body and push the ball. Head tilters have a habit of pushing the ball high and away from their target.

Avoid dropping your glove and tilting your head.

THE RELEASE

The primary objective during the release phase of the throwing action is to extend the ball and throwing arm out in front of your body. Generally speaking, the release point would be in a position around 10 or 11 o'clock.

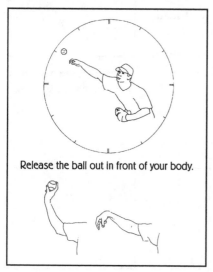

Release the ball out in front of your body.

Snap your wrist down through the ball.

The point of release should be well out in front of your body. Your arm should continue to accelerate right through this point. As your arm and ball approach the point of release, your arm should be close to extended, though not locked at the elbow. Locking your arm will cause short-arming of the ball, which cheats your velocity. Full extension, as far as you can reach, will not happen until after your release. Let the extension be natural, without recoiling your arm.

Be out in front when you release to ensure strong, low throws and avoid "rainbows." A ball lofted in a high arc can only be caught when it returns to earth, so your throw should be on a straight line. Even if the throw is short and bounces, it can be caught more easily.

Your forearm will lead the ball through the release point as your wrist is cocked and the ball now faces the sky. This will occur naturally as your body rotates so long as the ball was properly facing away at the "T" position. Once your arm arrives at the desired point of release, your wrist will quickly snap forward and down. This wrist action can generate anywhere from three to six additional miles per hour on the throw.

THE FOLLOW-THROUGH

Follow through after you release the ball.

The proper follow-through procedure should be a natural finish. Don't *force* your arm to go the entire route. Rather, make the process an act of muscle memory.

There are three distinct checkpoints during the follow-through. First, after the release and extension, your throwing hand will follow a route outside the stride knee and touch a point on the glove side of your body. Slapping your side means that your arm has completed the entire throwing route. As this happens, the back of your throwing shoulder should be visible to the target.

MAC FACT: *Slap your glove side with your throwing hand to make sure that your arm has completed the entire route.*

Second, trunk rotation will continue so that your head finishes out in front of your lead knee and foot. Your back should be at an angle, not straight up and down. Your body will be bent at the waist so that your upper body is horizontal.

Third, exploding your hips will have forced your back foot to pop up and release from its position. Make sure that the back of your body comes forward at least even with your stride foot. Don't leave your back foot planted on the ground in the same spot it began the throwing process.

THE GRIP and ROTATION

The proper grip on the baseball is a four-seam grip. While the ball will be touching most of your first two fingers, the pressure will be administered by the pads of your fingers and thumb. The pads of your first two fingers will be on a seam. A small space, the width of another finger, should be between the two fingers. Young players especially have a tendency to spread their fingers too far apart. Your thumb should be directly underneath the space between your two fingers. With your fingers and thumb positioned correctly, if you turned the baseball you would notice that four seams will rotate.

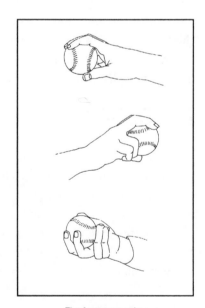

The four-seam grip.

Your ring (third) and pinky (little) fingers should naturally curl into the palm of your hand. Small players may have to consider using a third finger until their hands grow. Make sure there is a space between the palm of your hand and the ball. Don't choke the baseball by holding it deep in your palm. Holding the ball out on your fingertips allows the wrist to generate more speed.

Your fingers should be placed on the seam in the middle of the ball. Don't let your thumb or fingers move too far to one side. You want to throw the entire baseball. This may sound obvious, but take note that if your fingers range too far either way, you are only throwing half the ball.

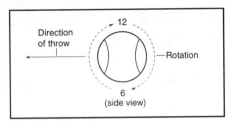

The proper rotation of the four-seam grip.

When gripped properly, the thrown ball should rotate so that the spin moves in a rotation from 12 o'clock to 6 o'clock. This spin is called true or four-seam rotation. Coaches can watch for a small dot caused by the seams on the ball spinning incorrectly. This dot demonstrates poor rotation, probably caused by an inefficient grip. Balls thrown with four-seam rotation will travel the fastest and straightest route. In addition, if the ball bounces, a four-seamer will skip straight up, and not scoot left or right.

MAC FACT: *The goal is four-seam rotation on every throw.*

Throwing a baseball appears to be an easy task. Indeed, for many players it's as easy as it looks. For many others, however, an accurate throw rarely happens. Because the throwing motion is a habit, it becomes more difficult to make changes to a player's delivery as he or she ages. This highlights the importance of encouraging healthy training habits in the early years.

Coaches might consider beginning each practice or pregame session with two or three of the throwing drills described in this chapter. Pick the most appropriate warm-up for a given day. By changing the drills on a regular basis you can add variety to your practices and work on different mechanical aspects of throwing.

ARM STRENGTH

If you live in the right climate, you have ready access to the outdoors in February and can begin preparing for the season early. However, living in a less accommodating climate need not hinder your preparation for the coming baseball season. Set up a hockey net in the laundry room, hang a piece of carpet in the garage, toss a lacrosse ball against a brick wall. The point is to make sure you start throwing as early as possible in order to develop optimum arm strength for the games ahead. On the other hand, be sure to rest your arm when fatigue sets in. Injury and bad throwing habits often occur near the end of long drills when players are tired.

MAC FACT: *A daily throwing regime will increase arm strength dramatically.*

THROWING DRILLS

#1 — FLICK DRILL

Objective: To practice good wrist action.
             To observe good rotation of the baseball.

Setup: Players set up with a partner or a target at a distance of 7 to 10 feet, with one baseball.

Procedure: Apply a proper four-seam grip to the ball. Your glove will support your throwing elbow at chest height. Your elbow will be bent 90 degrees. Cock your wrist so the ball faces the sky. The ball should be in a position above eye level. From this starting position, flick the ball to the target using only your wrist.

Flick Drill

Coach's Note: Make sure the player does not use his whole arm to throw the ball. The focus is solely on the wrist to generate the proper rotation and to promote a good firm snap. Standing behind the player to observe the rotation, make sure the ball is spinning in a 12 o'clock to 6 o'clock rotation. Gradually encourage the player to generate more power from the wrist.

Variation: This drill is also effective for pitchers as they develop new pitches such as the curve ball or circle change.

#2 — ONE-KNEE DRILL

Objective: To practice finishing the arm route.
             To develop good follow through.

Setup: Players set up with a partner or a target at a distance of 7 to 10 feet, with one baseball.

Procedure: Begin with your throwing-side knee on the ground. The glove-side knee will be bent at a 90-degree angle with your foot flat on the ground pointing at the target. Do not let your bent leg wander. Your upper body should be erect. Don't sit back on your heel. Start with hands

One-Knee Drill

together in the centre of your body, then break with your thumbs down and proceed in slow motion up to the "T" position. From this starting position, begin accelerating your arm and release the ball out in front with your arm extending outside your lead knee to slap your side.

Coach's Note: Reinforce the hand break and a good "T." Make sure the player gets extension through the release point and finishes the arm route.

#3 — T DRILL

Objective: To become familiar with the proper throwing position.
To achieve a good follow-through.
To develop an efficient hand break.

Setup: Players set up with a partner or a target at a distance of about 30 feet, with one baseball.

Procedure: Start with your toes about shoulder-width apart, pointing at the target and with your knees flexed comfortably. With your hands together, rotate your shoulders and assume the "T" or throwing position. Continue your arm action and throw the baseball. Make sure that your arm and head are out in front of the body when you finish. Bend at the waist during the follow-through. Your feet will remain stationary throughout the drill in order to isolate your upper body and your throwing-arm action.

"T" Drill

Coach's Note: If the player stumbles forward due to excess momentum, this is preferable to the opposite. Check to see if the player assumes the proper throwing position with the ball facing away and the throwing elbow at or above the shoulder.

Variation: If the player has trouble accomplishing a good throwing position, break the drill into two steps. First, have him slowly rotate to the "T" position and stop. Then, from the throwing position he can continue the delivery. This variation institutes another check to make sure the mechanical process is solid before proceeding with the entire arm action.

#4 — TWO BALL DRILL

Objective: To concentrate on the role of the glove side.

Setup: Players set up with a partner or a target at a distance of about 30 feet, with two baseballs.

Procedure: This drill follows the same procedure as the T Drill. The only difference is that you will use two baseballs. One you will throw, the other you will hold in your glove during the drill. As you practice this drill, you must concentrate on the glove side or else the ball will fall out.

Coach's Note: The extra ball encourages the player to control the glove side during the throw.

Variation: The two-ball concept can be instituted into the other drills also. Remember that when you use two balls it will change the focus of the drill. I do not encourage making players concentrate on too many things at once when going through mechanical drills. Only use the two balls when you want your players to focus solely on the role of their glove side.

#5 — FORCED STRIDE DRILL

Objective: To concentrate on the role of the lower body during the follow-through.
To become familiar with a comfortable stride point.

Setup: Players set up with a partner or a target at a distance of about 40 feet, with one baseball.

Procedure: Start with your back foot squared and your stride foot at a comfortable distance. The toes of the stride foot should be pointed at the target or closed (so that the outside of the foot is directed at the target). Your weight should be evenly distributed on the balls of your feet. Your head should be aligned with the centre of your body. Start with your hands together and break in a slow motion up to the "T" position before accelerating to the release point. Your back leg should release from the ground and pop up as the ball is released. Your head and throwing arm should be in front of the rest of your body as you finish the arm route.

Forced Stride Drill

Coach's Note: Observe good balance before allowing the player to throw the ball. Check to see that the lower body continues to finish the throwing process. The back foot should not remain planted.

Variation: As players become proficient at this drill, change the focus by teaching the concept of hip explosion as a means of generating more force behind throws.

#6 — SKIP and THROW DRILL

Objective: To learn to take a positive step towards the target.
To develop the momentum necessary in the throwing process.

Setup: Players set up with a partner or a target at a distance of 45 feet, with one baseball. The distance should gradually be increased during the drill.

Procedure: Start in a sideways position so that the directional side is already established. Your left side (right-handers) will face the target. Your hands begin together. Flex your knees comfortably. From this starting position, pick up your back foot and cross in front to square it to the target. The stride will follow, thus initiating the throwing process.

Skip & Throw Drill

Coach's Note: Force players to step in front. Remind players of the importance of good balance for the sake of control and accuracy. Encourage players with better balance to take a quicker step in front so that they can get rid of the ball more quickly.

#7 — ONE HOP DRILL

Objective: To achieve proper ball rotation.

Setup: Players set up with a baseball, and either a partner or target. The distance between them should be that of a throw across the diamond.

Procedure: Start with your toes and body facing the target, and hands together. Take a positive step by lifting your throwing side foot and squaring it in front. You should try to cover some distance with this step. Throw the ball on one hop to the target.

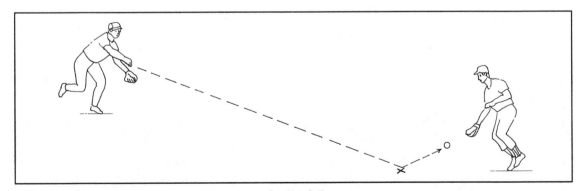

One Hop Drill

Coach's Note: Watch the skip the ball takes. If it skips straight, then the player had good rotation. Correct the grip or arm action if the hop veers to the left or right.

#8 — CROWHOP DRILL

Objective: To teach the proper footwork of a crowhop step which is essential for developing momentum and power behind a throw.

Setup: The same as with the One Hop Drill but increase the distance.

Procedure: Start with your toes and body facing the target. Place your baseball hat on the ground about a foot in front. Right-handed throwers will push off on their left foot and land over the hat on their right foot. Left-handers will push off with their right foot and land on their left. When you land, your foot should be squared and your body turned to the directional side as you continue the throwing process. Once again, righties push off their left foot to hop over the hat and land on the right foot, squared, and throw the ball. Vice versa for lefties.

Crowhop Drill

Coach's Note: If you have never tried this before, then practice yourself so that you can demonstrate. The first time you introduce this drill you should have players practice without a ball. Once players understand the footwork involved, have them throw the ball. It is very important that players don't take a skip step. In other words, they do not push off and land on the same foot. It is a hop, from one foot to the other. As they become familiar with the drill, switch the focus to explosive power to generate more distance on each throw.

#9 – MOVE'EM BACK DRILL

Objective: To become efficient at taking a positive step.
To develop accurate throwing skills.
To have some fun.

Setup: Pair off players into equal teams; each team has a ball. One of the partners will start on the foul line, the other will begin about 25 feet away.

Procedure: The teams of two are competing against one another. All the baseballs start with the partner on the foul line. The coach commands "step and throw" and the players in unison throw the ball to their partner. The receiver or partner acts like a first baseman. If he cannot catch the ball without moving his feet, then that pair is removed from the contest. After each partner makes an accurate throw, the player not on the foul line will move further back. Move back by two giant steps each time. This drill continues until only one team is left.

Coach's Note: Do not let players get away with poor mechanics, especially negative steps. Disqualify them immediately. As the distance increases, encourage the use of a crowhop. Perhaps you can offer a reward to the winners, even if that reward is less conditioning.

Variation: If you wish to promote good receiving skills (next chapter), then you can allow the partner to move her feet to catch the ball. This decision depends on your goal for that day — accurate throws or a combination of receiving and throwing skills.

#10 – BUCKET DRILL

Objective: To develop accuracy.
To practice the crowhop in a game-like situation.
To have some fun.

Setup: Place a large garbage pail or bucket on its side at home plate so that the hole is open to the playing field. Split the players into two teams. Arrange one team just left of second base in the outfield, the other team will be in a line just right of second base.

Procedure: The coach stands between the two teams behind second base. The first player stands in the middle facing the coach and the target. The coach will toss the ball straight up in the air.

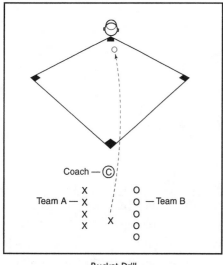

Bucket Drill

The player must catch the ball and then take a crowhop to throw the ball towards the bucket. If the ball goes in, your team gets two points. If the ball hits any part of the bucket, it is worth one point.

Coach's Note: Try to make the teams as even as possible. Make the contest worth something. Disqualify bad footwork.

Variation: Adjust the distance according to the age group.

#11 — CLOSED EYES DRILL

Objective: To promote good overall mechanics.
To generate accurate throws.

Setup: Players set up with either a partner or a target and one baseball. Start with a distance of about 40 feet.

Procedure: Start with your hands together and toes pointed at the target. Shut your eyes, take a positive step, and begin the throwing process. Follow through to complete the action.

Coach's Note: If players are throwing to a partner, stress that only the thrower will shut his eyes, not the receiver! Gradually increase the distance.

Variation: As the player throws the ball, have them call out whether they think it was an accurate throw. They can simply yell "yes" if it was on target, or "no" if it was not. This calling out helps players to get a feel for their throws. This drill can be incorporated with the other drills, but take note that it may impact the goal or objective of that drill.

SECOND INNING
RECEIVING THE BASEBALL

RECEIVING THE BASEBALL

Once someone has thrown the ball, that ball needs to be caught. Yet, catching the baseball is not as simple as it appears. When Devon White makes a basket catch at his waist or Ricky Henderson snaps the glove after taking in a fly ball, the casual observer thinks it is the simplest task in all of sports. What the average fan does not realize is that both Ricky and Devon perform several important movements in order to make that catch. That they also add some flair to the action can be attributed to their entertainment skills as major league players.

Getting to the ball quickly and moving into proper position will simplify the art of receiving the baseball. Proper receiving can also eliminate the effects of bad throws. Remember: In order to make a play in the field, there is one throw and one catch. If the throw is imperfect, the player in good position can catch the ball and make adjustments in order to complete the play. All too often, the receiver expects a perfect throw and is not prepared for one that is slightly off.

MAC FACT: *Always expect a bad throw!*

If you think a bad throw is on its way, then you should be ready to adjust your position and turn a poor throw into a successful out. The receiving and throwing component of many plays are often equally to blame when errors result. However, the ultimate blame usually falls to the player who makes the errant toss.

At the start of practice and during pregame warm-ups, proper receiving mechanics are as important as throwing form and deserve equal attention. Just because players are working on getting their arms loose doesn't mean they can neglect improvement of receiving mechanics. Every repetition of a bad habit takes many more quality repetitions to correct. Do not let poor work habits or lack of coaching supervision during throwing drills condition you into becoming a poor receiver. Don't convince yourself that you can approach the receiving aspect nonchalantly during practice and then perform at the highest level during the game. Muscles remember. When the game is on the line and you don't have time to think — only react — it's your responsibility to ensure that those muscles remember the proper way to catch the ball, because that's how you practice each and every time.

MAC FACT: *Habits developed during practice will carry over into the game.*

Receiving the baseball requires athletic movements on the part of the player. You must begin in a balanced and mobile position with flexed knees. Your feet will be slightly apart and staggered. Your hands will be in front of the body, ready to cushion the ball as it's being caught. Every throw should be caught in the centre of your body with two hands. Quick feet are necessary to get to the ball quickly and then, once the ball is caught, to move into proper throwing position.

POSITIONING OF THE FEET AND BODY

When you're prepared to catch a ball, your feet should be positioned about shoulder-width apart with the knees flexed. Point the toes slightly outward so that your feet are opened. Opening the feet enables you to react quickly to a poorly thrown ball. The feet will be slightly staggered so that the back foot (throwing side) is about two inches behind the other. Don't stagger the feet too much and allow the shoulders to become uneven. Your shoulders must be square to the ball.

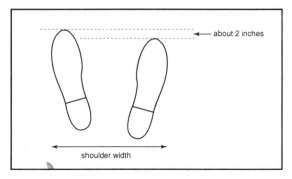

Positioning of the feet to receive the ball.

Weight is best distributed evenly on the balls of the feet. You have assumed an athletic position, and you should be both comfortable and mobile.

The receiver's body should be positioned in line with the ball, glove, and the body of the person throwing the ball. Setting your body in this position should enable you to receive every throw in the centre of your body. Your first objective, whenever possible, is to catch the ball in the centre of your body with both hands.

MAC FACT: *Catch every throw in the centre of the body.*

THE HANDS

Both hands should be extended in front of the body about twelve inches, and your elbows should be flexed. Always use two hands to catch the ball. The use of both hands will enable you to cushion the ball as you are catching it. The throwing hand prevents the ball from slipping out and is ready to begin the transfer from receiving position to throwing position.

MAC FACT: *Always use two hands to catch the ball.*

If the ball is thrown above the waist, the hands should be in a position so that the thumbs are touching. If the ball is thrown below the waist, the pinky fingers should touch. As you catch the ball, begin to cradle it into the belly button with both hands. This concept of cradling the ball is called "soft hands." Soft hands are a necessity for all infielders. Players can develop soft hands by concentrating during throwing drills on eliminating any sound when catching the ball. The quieter you can receive the ball, the softer your hands.

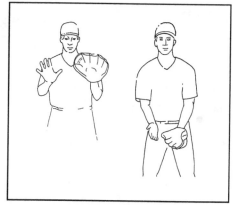

Both hands extended in front of the body.

Receiving throws above the waist (left) and below the waist (right).

QUICKNESS OF THE FEET

Always move your feet to the ball first, rather than the glove. If your feet are in a good position, then it becomes much easier to catch the ball or to adjust if needed. Stay on the balls of your feet to avoid getting caught flat-footed. Good receivers make or break bad throwers. Bad receivers, on the other hand, put a lot of pressure on the person throwing the ball to make a perfect throw every time.

Expecting a bad throw puts a receiver in a good frame of mind to react to the baseball. If you expect to move, then you can become more agile and get a good jump on the ball. Remember that your feet control your direction and positioning — not your glove.

GETTING TO THE THROWING POSITION

Once you have caught the ball, cradle it to your belly button — your centre of gravity — with both hands. This is the starting position for throwing the baseball, as discussed in the previous chapter. Once the ball has correctly been cradled into your body, your footwork is the most important action.

Your feet will initiate a quick, positive step towards the target while breaking your hands in order to throw the baseball. This transfer from the receiving process to the throwing phase is essential for making plays during a game. Stress the importance of quick feet and quick hands throughout the receiving process right through until the player has released the baseball.

Cradle the ball to initiate the throwing action.

OVERVIEW

One of the problems players confront when striving to develop good receiving skills is an oversized glove. For some reason, bigger is often associated with better. While it is true that a large glove might enable the player to cover a little more area, it is also true that it can harm the player's overall baseball skills.

Large gloves may cheat players out of the development of quick feet by convincing them they can reach for everything that comes their way. Furthermore, players may not develop quick hands because the ball gets lost in a big glove. When purchasing a glove, select one not much bigger than the player's own hand. She should feel the ball in the glove. This feel for the ball will allow the player to develop quick hands and reinforce the importance of using both hands to catch.

The goal of teaching and practicing receiving skills is to develop good habits. These habits are formed during drill and practice sessions. If a player makes two hundred throws a week, then he must catch the ball an equal number of times. If he only uses one hand during those catches, then expect him to use only one hand in a game. You cannot expect players to turn on good habits just because it's game time. Concentrating on good habits will carry over into the game as a result of muscle memory.

For younger players, fear is an element that must not be overlooked. If a player is afraid of the ball, he will never develop good receiving mechanics. Have these players start by using "soft touch" baseballs. If he does get hit with the ball, damage will be minimal and the player can continue. Eventually, he will gain confidence in his own abilities and with this renewed confidence, fear and timidity around the ball will diminish. Do not let players with fear escape or hide during throwing drills. Help them to overcome this problem. They may have to work harder and longer than the others.

RECEIVING DRILLS

It is important to stress receiving mechanics during throwing drills. Make sure players stay mentally focused and concentrate on the skills.

#1 — EGG TOSS DRILL

Objective: To learn how to cradle the ball.
To use two hands to catch.

Setup: You need at least one egg per player. Have the players partner up and have one egg between them. Gloves are not used for this drill.

Procedure: The first player with the egg will toss it underhand to his partner. The receiver will catch the egg with both hands and cradle it to his belly button. He, in turn, will throw it back to his partner. After each partner has made a successful catch, they move back a few steps and continue. As the distance increases, the egg may have to be thrown overhand.

Coach's Note: It is imperative that you stress to players that they must catch the egg in the centre of the body. Often the players will catch the egg at the side because they do not want to get splashed.

Variation: You can also use water balloons.

#2 — THE PADDLE DRILL

Objective: To reinforce the importance of using two hands.
To develop soft hands.

Setup: Make paddles for each player. Paddles are a piece of plywood cut into the shape of a mitten just a little bigger than the hand (see diagram). Pieces of dressmaker's elastic are screwed on to the paddle to serve as finger holes. Wooden paddles, as well as a foam version, are available at retail stores, but it's easy and cheaper to make your own.

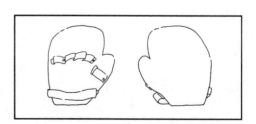

The paddle, used to develop soft hands.

Procedure: Position the players in a square about 10 feet apart, each with a paddle on her glove hand. Have them throw the ball around the square as quickly as possible. If they become bored, or extremely adept, add another baseball.

Coach's Note: Stress the importance of quick feet in terms of getting to the ball and getting rid of the ball. Since there is no pocket to catch the ball, players must use both hands. For this reason, the paddle drill is very effective at teaching players to use both hands to receive the ball. Furthermore, the wooden structure

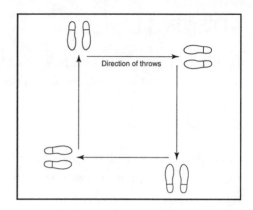

Paddle Drill

of the paddle is not conducive to cushioning a baseball, so in order to catch the ball silently, the player is forced to exaggerate the cradling action which helps to develop soft hands.

Variation: You may want to begin the drill with a soft touch baseball. You can start in a square or have players partner up instead. If using the square format, be sure to send the ball in different directions.

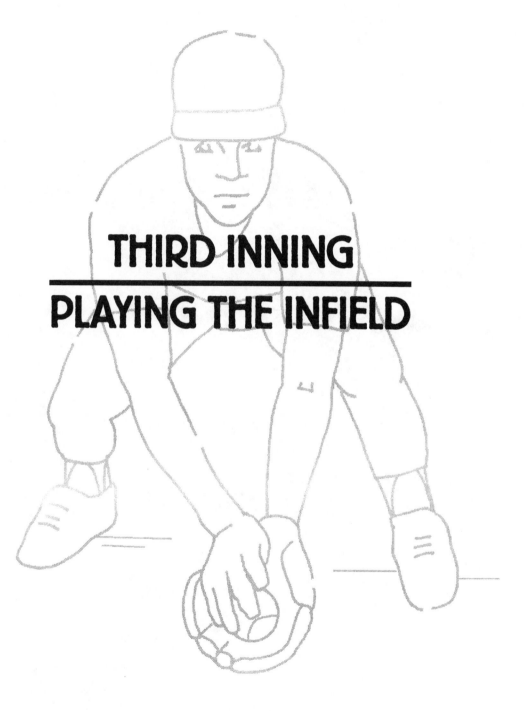

THIRD INNING
PLAYING THE INFIELD

PLAYING THE INFIELD

Most young players prefer the infield when choosing a defensive position. If they become skilled at their position, good defense can reduce the number of hits and runs in a game. Quite simply, good defense can win baseball games. So why don't players work on this area more frequently? I've witnessed many players who would not hesitate to take two hundred swings in a day. But, at the same time, they avoid fielding ground balls. Similarly, I've observed coaches who spend two hours on batting practice while devoting just ten minutes to infield drills.

The key to improving defensive skills is no secret. You must work at your position, become familiar with your surroundings, and commit yourself to many repetitions per day. These practice sessions should cover every situation that could arise in an actual game: slow rollers, hard smashes, balls to the left and right, pop-ups, double plays, and plays at the plate. It isn't necessary to practice every situation all the time; it *is* essential to keep your reaction times fresh so that you're prepared for any situation on the day of the big game. On a busy day, the middle infielders may receive six or eight opportunities to make a play. Those few chances alone are not enough to keep the defensive player sharp.

THE READY POSITION

Most errors are the result of poor preparation. You must prepare your feet for every pitch. Pitch preparation requires mental toughness and discipline. If the defensive team is on the field for 120 to 160 pitches every game, they have to discipline themselves to be ready on each and every pitch. Never make assumptions about where the next ball will be hit. It's the coach's responsibility to check the footwork of

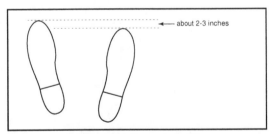

about 2-3 inches

Put your feet in the ready position.

each infielder, perhaps delegating this task to an assistant. Young players especially will be more conscientious about their footwork if they know that coaches are watching for it.

The feet should be slightly staggered and in an open position. Don't begin with your feet straight, because they will have to turn to move to the ball. The knees should be flexed, with the weight on the balls of your feet. Each player should find her individual comfort level in the ready position. Strive for an athletic, and agile, ready position.

The ready position is a necessary component of your fielding responsibilities, enabling you to begin in a position allowing immediate reaction to any batting scenario. Flexed knees keep the lower body loose and relaxed, and capable of an explosive first step to go get the ball. This preparation prior to the pitch is essential for you to be "ready" to field the ball.

As middle infielders (shortstop and second baseman) you will be somewhat erect, instead of crouched low. Few balls are hit directly at middle infielders, making it more likely that you will have to move to field the ball. It isn't useful or effective to begin in a crouch, come up before moving to the ball, and then crouch again.

Since first and third basemen are closer to the hitter, they start lower to the ground. Ground balls have a tendency to arrive quicker at the corner positions. In addition, these positions have less field to cover and do not range as far to pick up balls.

Watch the ball enter the hitting zone and then prepare your feet. Preparing your feet can be accomplished several ways. "Explode" the feet with a little hop-step as the ball enters the hitting zone. Be sure the weight is distributed on the balls of your feet so that you're in position to pivot in any direction. Another method is a combination of creep steps. Creep with the right foot, and then the left as the ball enters the hitting zone. Some fielders prefer to step with the left, right, and then back to the left foot. Regardless of the footwork, you should rock forward for momentum. Most importantly, as an infielder you are "de-cleating," or lifting your cleats out of the ground on every pitch. De-cleating establishes momentum prior to the actual play, increasing your reaction time to the ball. While you begin these prepatory steps prior to the ball entering the hitting zone, it is essential that both feet are back down on the ground when contact is made so that you are ready to move to the ball.

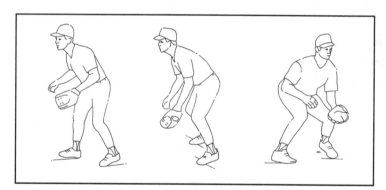

Prepare your feet by "de-cleating."

MAC FACT: *De-cleating is essential on every pitch.*

Let comfort decide what you do with your hands while in the ready position. Some players will have their hands together, with the bare hand tucked inside the glove. Others will leave their hands at their sides. In either case, your palms should be facing up with your glove open. Be sure to establish good foot preparation. Stay loose and relaxed, but prepared to respond with a controlled explosion when the ball goes into play.

MOVING TO THE BALL

Once the ball has been hit, move aggressively. Close the distance between yourself and the ball as quickly as possible, allowing time to get into the proper fielding position. Keep hands in front of the body while making your approach.

If the ball is hit left, pivot the left foot (the one closest to the ball) so that the toes are pointing in the direction you wish to move. Cross over with the right foot. This pivot-crossover step allows you to cover more distance with the first step. Avoid the jab step at this point, that is, moving the left foot first in a short stride or jab about half the distance of a normal step. As far as distance and speed are concerned, this move is less efficient than the pivot-crossover step. Your objective is to cover as much ground as possible with the first movement.

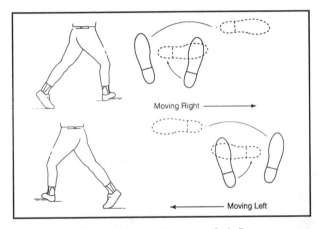

Moving Right ⟶

Moving Left ⟵

Pivot and crossover to move to the ball.

MAC FACT: *Move to the ball with a pivot-crossover step.*

Similarly, on balls hit to your right, pivot on the right foot and cross over with the left. After the pivot-crossover step, your shoulders should be turned to face the direction you're heading. Don't run with your shoulders facing the hitting area. This running form will slow you down. Position your body properly while moving to the ball similar to the way you would run on a base hit. Run towards the spot where the ball is headed, then turn and square up to the ball in order to field it most effectively.

Keep your body at the same height as when you began. Avoid standing up to run; stay slightly crouched instead.

FIELDING POSITION

Having positioned yourself for the ball, your task is to prepare your body to receive it. Feet should be slightly staggered. Your throwing-side foot will be about 2 inches behind the glove-side foot. Shoulders must be square to the ball. Staggering your feet excessively will angle the shoulders, causing the ball to bounce off sideways. Keeping shoulders square increases the chances the ball will fall in front of you, where it will be that much easier to pick up and complete the play.

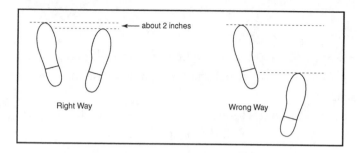

MAC FACT: *Keep the shoulders square at all times when fielding the ball.*

Avoid staggering your feet too much so that you are not square to the ball.

Bend your knees so that your thighs are parallel to the ground. Distribute your weight over the balls of your feet to maintain good balance.

Your hands should be out in front of your body with the elbows slightly flexed, not locked. The farther in front that your hands can extend to field the ball, the easier it is to watch the ball enter the glove. Your goal is to field the ball at the "top of the triangle." If you draw a

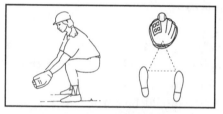

Extend your hands out front to field at the top of the triangle.

triangle in the infield dirt using your feet as the bottom two points of the triangle, it is easier to observe the vital relationship between hands and feet.

MAC FACT: *Field the ball at the top of the triangle.*

One of the most common fielding mistakes is attempting to catch the ball after it has dropped too low or deep. Your field of vision is restricted, for instance, if you let the ball get to the point where it is between your feet. If not fielded cleanly, it becomes difficult to handle the ball and it ends up behind you. Everyone has seen this happen: The fielder circling while looking for the booted ball, and perhaps even kicking it further away. This is the result of trying to field ground balls too deep in your body, so be sure you've got your hands out in front.

Position your hands palm to palm, with the throwing hand on top of the glove. With your bare hand in this position, your face is protected in the event of a bad hop. The majority of bad ball hops go either up or down, very seldom sideways.

Field the ball with your hands in a palm-to-palm relationship.

MAC FACT: *Position hands palm to palm.*

Hands should also be positioned in the centre of your body. Try to avoid fielding the ball too far to one side or the other. You can cover more area and be a wider backstop by fielding balls in the centre. Also, the glove hand has greater mobility when it begins in the middle of the body.

As a fielder, your head is your guide. Head and eyes will follow the ball right to your glove. As the ball enters the glove, your head should be tilted so that the button on the the top of your hat is showing. Don't over anticipate the ball into the glove or peek too soon. You can't throw anyone out until you've solidly caught the ball.

SOFT HANDS and QUICK FEET

"Soft hands and quick feet" are the goals of all infielders. You will always hear a professional scout commenting on a player's hands. The hands are the prime measurable tool of an infielder. Quick feet are essential if a ball is not fielded cleanly, for turning the double play, and to offset the advantage gained by a speedy runner.

Soft hands can be developed through practice and the development of proper technique. As the ball enters the glove, you should initiate a cradling or cushioning motion by bringing the outstretched hands into the belly button. This cradling movement reduces ball impact. Players with soft hands can often be identified by listening to how they field the ball. Soft hands will take away the loud crack that is heard when the ball hits the glove. One of the keys to developing this skill is to make sure that your hands are extended out in front of the body when fielding the ball. If the hands are too far back, you've decreased the space available for cushioning the ball.

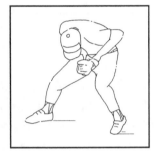

Cradle the ball to your belly button.

MAC FACT: *Infielders must develop soft or silent hands — "fielding quietly."*

As the ball is caught and brought into your belly button, feet dominate the movements. Quick feet enable you to move from a fielder to a thrower in as short a transition time as possible. While cradling the ball, initiate foot movement by taking a positive step to the target with your throwing-side foot. This positive step will promote good direction as your body turns sideways to achieve proper throwing position.

If you're a young or inexperienced player, be attentive during this transition from fielding position to throwing position. Remember to solidly catch the ball before you throw it. Avoid setting your body up for the throw before the ball is under control. By turning your body too soon, the ball may bounce off of you and too far away to make the play. Young or inexperienced players should take the ball to their belly buttons, the body's centre of gravity, and then take the positive step.

Older, more experienced players are encouraged to make a quicker and smoother transition. As the ball hits the glove, your feet will begin to position the body to throw. With practice and drill, players can become very adept at developing quick feet. As a coach I constantly reinforce this for infielders by calling out, "Soft hands, quick feet!"

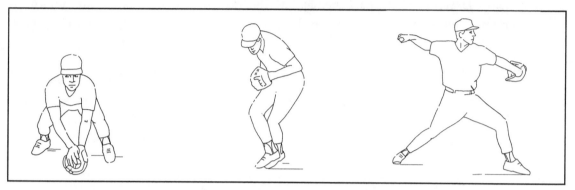

Quick feet transform the fielder into a thrower.

Having received the ball and achieved proper body position, let's examine the throwing action of an infielder. Infielders should not take a full arm circle when throwing the baseball. Their goal is to cut the arc in half. The shortening of the arm route will allow them to release the ball quicker. Normally, when you take the ball out of the glove, it will go down to waist level before completing the circle back up and behind the head. As an infielder, take the ball out of the glove and go straight back to the point of arm extension without dropping the arm down to the waist. This modification of the throwing mechanics offers a quicker release and gives you an advantage on close plays.

MAC FACT: *Infielders should cut the arm circle in half to gain a quicker release.*

Infielders use a short, quick arm circle.

Quite often middle infielders develop a lower release point. In other words, they have a tendency to drop their elbow when releasing the ball. This release point, or arm slot, results from the fielder shortening the arm route and trying to release the ball more quickly. Better that this action occur naturally rather than forcing a drop in your elbow to make the throw. Notice, however, how a shortstop might handle the ball when deep in the hole between short and third. He will always throw it over the top with a large arm circle in order to increase the power of the throw. This action tells you that your arm strength lies in releasing the ball from a higher arm slot. Also, you will notice that third basemen avoid dropping their arm to throw. They employ a large arm circle and cut loose with good arm strength. Follow suit and let this occur naturally.

There is an advantage to throwing the ball by dropping the elbow. That advantage is the movement on the ball. A ball thrown from a high arm slot will vary up or down. A ball thrown from a lower arm slot will vary to the left or right of the target. If an infielder makes an errant throw, a left or right adjustment has a larger margin for error so the first baseman can still complete an out. However, if the ball is thrown too high or low, chances are greater that an error will result.

FIELDING BUNTS

When fielding bunts or any ball without momentum, the lower body once again plays an important role. By employing certain tactics, you can easily turn a bunt into an out.

Your first objective is to approach the ball, straddling it so that your feet are lined up with the target. In other words, set the feet in the throwing position. With the ball now located in the centre of your body, scoop it up with two hands. Don't attempt to field the ball too close to either one of your feet because if mishandled, the ball will have covered too much ground to recover in time to get the out. Use two hands to field the ball. Too many infielders who pick the ball up with their bare hand develop a bad habit of patting the glove before they throw. This action of patting the glove, taking the ball back in the glove and then out again, loses precious time. Losing even fractions of a second can make the difference on a possible bang-bang play at first base.

MAC FACT: *Set the feet to the target and stand directly over the ball.*

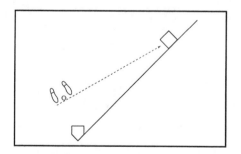

Set your feet to the target.

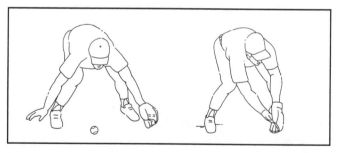

Scoop the ball with both hands.

MAC FACT: *Field the ball with two hands by scooping it into the belly button.*

Once you've correctly fielded the ball, you're in good position to complete the throw. If you have time, you can take a positive step to the target. If the play is close, throwing from that position shouldn't be a problem since you've already established good direction and balance.

TAGGING RUNNERS

There are two methods for an infielder to tag a runner — a pop tag and a sweep tag. When using either method of applying a tag on a runner, you should follow certain rules. Don't reach for the runner. If the runner is sliding in to your base there's no point reaching out to try a tag. Instead, position the glove in front of the base and let the runner slide into it. Let the runner come to you. Once you've applied the tag, snatch the ball and glove out of the way to safety. Make the tag, avoid injury, and keep the ball safely in the glove. The longer you leave the glove and ball in the path of the sliding runner, the greater the opportunity for the ball to come loose or an injury to occur.

MAC FACT: *Do not reach for runners; let them come to you.*

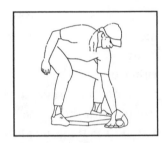

Put the tag down in front of the bag and let the runner slide into it; do not reach for the runner.

For a sweep tag, it's essential that you receive the ball with your glove in front of the base. As you receive the ball, let the momentum in the ball carry the glove down in front of the base in a sweeping motion. Don't receive the ball behind the base: if the runner arrives before the ball, the ball might strike him, then bounce away allowing an extra base. Also, the momentum of the ball is strong. Catching the ball behind the base makes it more difficult to stop the ball, then bring it back to the base to complete the tag. And if the ball is moving away, the action to bring it back is much slower. Instead, use the momentum of the ball itself to assist with the tag.

MAC FACT: *During a sweep tag, receive the ball in front of the base and let the momentum take the glove to the base.*

A pop tag involves receiving the ball above the base and simply popping the glove down on the sliding runner and back up again out of the way. Again, you must catch the ball first, before you can apply the tag. All too often, players drop their head and glove to apply the tag before the ball has arrived. This increases the chances that the runner will make the base safely, and perhaps take another.

MAC FACT: *You must catch the ball first, then apply the tag.*

If the runner attempts to slide outside the baseline in an effort to avoid the tag, follow the shape of the base so that your glove is positioned to tag the runner once he moves for the base.

Remember, don't reach for the runner — if you are in the proper position, the runner must come to you.

POP-UPS

When a ball is hit straight up in the infield, there is always the question as to who should take responsibility and catch it. As an infielder, you must assume that you can catch every pop-up. The coach wants all of his infielders to be aggressive. However, someone must carry authority when the ball is in the air. That person asserts his or her authority by making a verbal command. Any command is acceptable — "mine," or "I got it." Whatever call you decide on, keep it simple and be consistent.

MAC FACT: *The player who wants the ball should use a loud verbal command to let the other fielders know she has it.*

You should yell in a dominant voice. Quiet voices can often result in unneeded collisions. Bark out if you are going to take the ball. Once someone asserts authority, the other fielders should clear the way. Generally speaking, the shortstop and catcher usually assume dominant roles in the infield. This trend is not written in stone. However, it is a good habit to have some form of defensive captain on the field. This person should have a loud voice and establish communications with the other players on the field.

Once the ball is hit, head toward it. Do not drift. Get to the spot and set up to catch the ball. Now, you can adjust according to the spin on the ball or the wind. Catch all pop-ups with two hands. Using two hands is particularly important because the spin on pop-ups is usually a very hard and tight rotation. This tight spin makes it easy for the ball to pop out of the glove. The bare hand is used to make sure the ball stays in the glove where you want it.

MAC FACT: *Always use two hands on pop-ups.*

Try to catch all pop-ups at or above eye level. This height will make it easier to watch the ball the entire way into your glove. Once an object drops below eye level, hand-eye co-ordination suffers. If an object is above or below eye level for the entire activity, problems are fewer. However, when objects cross the eye level, it becomes much more difficult to react.

Catch pop-ups with two hands above your head.

MAC FACT: *Try to catch the ball at or above eye level.*

The drop step: pivot and open up.

On balls hit softly over the infielder's head, employ a "drop step." A drop step involves two actions — pivot and open up. If a ball is hit over your right shoulder, pivot on your left foot. A pivot is the act of turning the foot on the balls of the feet so that the toes are now pointing sideways towards the other foot instead of to home plate. After the left foot pivots, the right foot will lift allowing your body to open up before stepping backwards in the direction your body needs to go. On balls hit over your left shoulder, you will pivot on your right foot and then open up the left foot and step towards the spot where the ball is going.

Keep in mind that your goal is to take the straightest, shortest, route to the ball. This first step, or drop step, is the key to getting a good jump on the ball. It is essential that you completely open up when performing this skill. The drop step should put you in a position whereby your body is now facing the direction you want to run. As you begin to run, your body will be facing the spot where the ball is heading. If you want to see the ball, you can do so by glancing over your shoulder. Don't turn the body back around in order to look at the ball, as this action will only slow you down. Glancing over the shoulder requires a turn of the head, and not a turn of the body.

MAC FACT: *Teach the drop step — an action that enables fielders to get a good positive first step and to take the shortest route to the ball.*

Once you have performed a drop step and are sprinting towards the ball, you must decide how much time you have. If time permits, you should position yourself under the ball with your body facing back to the infield and catch the ball with two hands. If, however, you don't have time, you may have to make a one-handed over-the-shoulder catch.

In summary, the following represent good infielding techniques:

- keep low to the ground
- balance weight on the balls of the feet
- keep square to the ball
- be "ready" on every pitch
- be prepared to move when the ball enters the hitting area

- maintain good balance
- use two hands
- field the ball at the "top of the triangle"
- position hands palm to palm
- cradle the ball to the centre of the body
- develop soft hands
- take a positive step to the throwing position
- have quick feet
- communicate with infield teammates — call for the ball during double plays and pop-ups
- cultivate strong, accurate throws

DOUBLE PLAYS BY A SHORTSTOP

The double play is the mark of a good defensive team. As the ball is hit, a fielder will make the play and throw the ball to second base (referred to as a "feed") where the shortstop or second baseman will receive the ball for the first out and then continue to throw the ball (referred to as the "pivot") to first base to complete the double play. The shortstop becomes the pivot man on any balls hit to the right side of the infield (first baseman and second baseman). The second baseman, on the other hand, will become the pivot man on any ground ball hit at the shortstop or third baseman.

Coaches should make a point of teaching pivots from both sides of second base to all middle infielders. Even if you intend to play shortstop all year, it is essential that you become familiar with how to turn a double play from the second base position in case of injury. The coach's job is to prepare his team for any situation. An inability to insert another player who can turn the pivot is lack of preparation. The same applies for second basemen. All middle infielders must learn the double play pivot from both sides of the bag.

MAC FACT: *All middle infielders should learn pivots from both sides of second base.*

The shortstop has the easier pivot when attempting a double play. Since she is moving towards second base from the shortstop position, momentum assists in establishing direction and affords a better opportunity to make a strong throw. Move across the field, leading up to the pivot as your body prepares to receive the ball, then throw it to first base. As you complete this skill, there is no need to check your body or change directions. Instead, use this momentum to your advantage.

Proper footwork is the key to turning the double play. To avoid tangling your feet and losing track of the ball, use a cue word or key phrase that is relatively simple and easy to remember when learning the pivot. If you approach the bag from left field side of the bag (i.e. shortstop), take your left foot to the ball. These cue words are key to learning the pivot.

As shortstop, get to the bag as early as possible and establish a straight line from the centre of your body over the base to the person throwing the ball. This positioning will offer the best target for the thrower. Both feet will start on the shortstop side of the base. Toes can be barely touching or reasonably close to the bag.

Shortstop pivot: Take your left foot to the ball.

Pop your hips around the corner to establish direction for your throw.

As the ball is thrown, the cue words come into play. From the left field side, take your left foot to the ball. Step over the base to the ball, then hop on both feet in such a manner that your feet are squared up and establishing good direction prior to throwing the ball. This hop as you receive the ball is referred to as "popping the hips around the corner" of the base.

MAC FACT: *As shortstop, take your left foot to the ball.*

The step to the ball involves timing, being comfortable, and loads of practice. Keep your left foot in the air (like the Karate Kid) until you determine the direction of the throw. Stepping too soon will limit your ability to save an errant throw. Anticipate a less than perfect throw. With your left foot in the air, observe where the throw is headed, and step in that direction.

MAC FACT: *Step to the ball once you know where the ball is going. Don't step too soon!*

"Popping the hips around the corner" is an action which sets up the direction for throwing. It enables you to get your feet, shoulders, and hips into the proper throwing position. Good throwing mechanics are as important as ever. A weak or wild throw could easily result in the batter getting an extra base.

MAC FACT: *Set the feet and establish direction before completing a throw.*

The concept of quick feet might be the crucial element for turning the pivot. Developing quick feet in other areas of the game will help complete double plays because of the improvement in accuracy and speed.

MAC FACT: *Quick feet can be the difference between a safe or out call.*

Use both hands to catch the ball. This way the throwing hand is ready to make the transfer. More experienced players need not worry about making contact with the base. If you get to the bag early to setup, and then step over the base to the ball, you will always get the call. Being too concerned over contact with the bag slows the pivot. In addition, shortstops should learn to cheat a little when completing the pivot. In other words, once you can see where the throw is headed, step to catch the ball early and clear the base. This places you closer to first base before throwing, creates a quicker release, and helps to avoid injury should the fielder have positioned herself further from the baseline depending on the direction of the throw. The entire movement should be so quickly done that it's hard to determine if your foot actually made contact with second base.

MAC FACT: *More experienced middle infielders should "cheat" slightly by clearing the base early.*

Another coaching tip for the shortstop is to try to catch every feed on the throwing side of the body. This can be achieved by taking a good first step to the ball. Receiving the throw on the throwing side will shorten the transfer time when taking the ball out of the glove, and thus quicken the release.

MAC FACT: *Step to the ball so that you can catch it on the throwing side of the body.*

SECOND BASEMEN TURNING THE DOUBLE PLAY

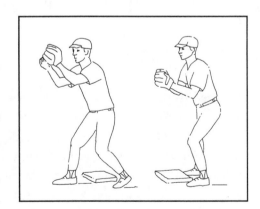

As a second baseman you face a more difficult task when completing the double play. Approach the bag, then stop and set up to make the throw in the direction from which you came. Remember, all of this must take place while a runner is barreling down upon you and trying to send you into left field.

As with the shortstop, a key word or phrase establishes the proper footwork for a second baseman. Because you're approaching from the right

Second baseman pivot: Take your right foot to the ball.

side of the field, take your right foot to the ball. The second baseman will approach the base and set up in a straight line with the base and person making the throw. Get to the base early and set up. As with the other pivot, place your toes near the bag. After observing the throw, step over the bag to the ball with your right foot. The left foot will naturally follow and should set up the appropriate direction for you to throw to first.

MAC FACT: *Approaching from the right side of the field, step with your right foot to the ball.*

Complete the pivot by striding towards first base and transferring your weight to the lead foot as you throw.

The throwing process is incomplete until the front foot lands. Attempting to throw with only one foot on the ground causes an off-balance, weak toss. Remember, you throw with both your feet. So the front foot must land before you can complete the pivot. While making the throw to first, transfer your weight to the front foot (the one closest to first base). With your weight on the front foot, you are more agile and able to avoid the oncoming runner.

MAC FACT: *Keep both feet on the ground prior to making the throw.*

MAC FACT: *Transfer the weight to your front foot to complete the throw.*

Certain aspects of the shortstop's pivot also apply to second basemen. Two hands are essential for a quick transfer. Quick feet will speed the release. Avoid closing the glove when receiving the ball. Finally, the first step should position the body so the ball can be caught on the throwing side.

SHORTSTOP FEEDS

The "feed" is the first half of a double play. The player who fields the ground ball will then feed, toss or flip it to the middle infielder who then attempts to complete the double play. It is useful to label the two main participants in a double combination in order to help define their roles. The person who fields the ground ball is known as the "sure guy." Her primary objective is to make sure that at least one player is called out. The key task for the sure guy is to make a good feed. The middle infielder who performs the pivot is called the "quick guy." If she is quick enough, the defence will increase its chances of completing the double play.

MAC FACT: *If you are making the feed, be certain of an out.*

There are four different feeds that are important to learn: Ground balls hit in your direction (a standard feed); balls hit between you and the base; plays which force you to go into the hole; and ground balls hit up the middle.

Balls hit in your direction, when you don't have to move too far left or right, are the easiest when it comes to completing a double play. Field the ball in the same way you would regular ground balls. The only difference is the positioning of your feet. When you know that you're going to feed the second baseman for a double play, set your feet so that they are staggered in the opposite manner than for normal ground balls. Your right heel will be even with the toes of your left foot. In this position, you will have opened up your entire body to the base.

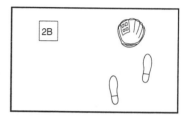

On standard feeds, open up to the base.

MAC FACT: *Stagger the feet and open up the body towards second base.*

The biggest mechanical changes occur once you have fielded the ball. Other than the feet, the actions to get the ball into the glove have not changed. The objective from this point on is to make a quick and accurate throw. The greatest priority is to complete the throw on target, but it is important to complete this throw in as little time as possible.

MAC FACT: *An accurate throw is the greatest priority.*

When you field the ball, your hands are usually at knee height or lower. Your rear end is also low since the fielding position requires the upper legs to be parallel to the ground. From this position, pivot on your right foot and lower your knee to the ground. While pivoting, be sure to clear the glove side. This involves dropping the glove or simply getting it out of the way. This

Once you have fielded the ball, drop the knee and throw across your body.

action is extremely beneficial to the second baseman (your double play partner) in terms of helping her see the ball. The glove can hide the ball and make it difficult to receive the feed.

MAC FACT: *Pivot, lower the knee near the ground, and clear the glove.*

At this stage, throw the ball across your body. The action is similar to completing a paintbrush stroke sideways from right to left. Dropping the arm slot and throwing across the body results in throws that will vary left or right. Again, inaccurate throws to the left or right are preferable to too high or too low. The second baseman will take his first step to the ball and can compensate for a wide throw and still complete the pivot. However, if your throw is too high or low, it becomes difficult to make the necessary adjustments and complete both outs.

MAC FACT: *Throw the ball across your body when making a feed.*

This feed by the shortstop is the one used most often during the game. It is a standard procedure that all middle infielders must be able to perform.

If your right foot is forward, pivot on the balls of your feet and complete the feed.

On ground balls in the hole between shortstop and third base, complete a pivot-crossover step to cut down the distance between you and the ball. If you can get to the ball and square up to field it properly, then you can complete the standard feed. If you must backhand the ball by turning your thumb over so that it points down, then your feed is dependent on which foot is closest to the ball when you field it.

If your right foot (throwing side) is closest to the ball, then you will stop your momentum, and pivot on the balls of your feet to turn the body and make the throw. At this point, the throwing mechanics are inconsequential. Remember, an accurate throw is the priority. Balls hit in the hole are the most difficult to turn into a double play. Thus it is imperative that the defence at least get the lead runner at second base.

If your left foot (glove side) is closest to the ball when it is caught, you will stop and take a power step back towards second base with the same foot (left). The right foot will pivot, assisting the power step. This step helps in establishing good direction and generates some momentum for your throw.

When making backhand plays, it is preferable to field the ball with your left foot forward. It is not always possible to do so, however, especially when your primary goal is to get to the ball.

On balls hit between you and second base, you should feed the second baseman an underhand flip toss. On these plays, you will be moving towards the base as you field the ball. Immediately after transferring the ball to the throwing hand, clear the glove to give the pivot man a clear view of the ball's source. Make an underhand flip toss, keeping your arm firm at the elbow. If your elbow bends, you may flip the ball over the head of the player awaiting the ball. The flip should be done with some authority, even though it is tossed underhand.

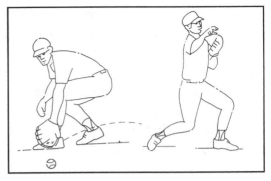

If your left foot is forward (the preferred footwork), step towards the base to complete the feed.

Get the ball into the second baseman's glove quickly and accurately. It is wise for middle infielders to practice together and get a feel for individual habits and preferences.

MAC FACT: *Keep the arm firm when making a flip; avoid bending the elbow.*

Finally, after completing the flip, follow your throw in case it is tossed over the second baseman's head. Since the second baseman is coming to the bag from the opposite direction, his momentum is taking him towards the left side of the field. You would get to the ball quicker because of your momentum in the event of an errant toss.

MAC FACT: *Follow your flip toss in case of a bad feed.*

A ball hit up the middle is perhaps the most difficult play to make. If you are running hard to prevent the ball from reaching the outfield, your body and momentum are moving towards right-centre field and away from the base. As you field the ball with one hand, quickly get the ball into your throwing hand and complete a backhanded flip to the second baseman. On a

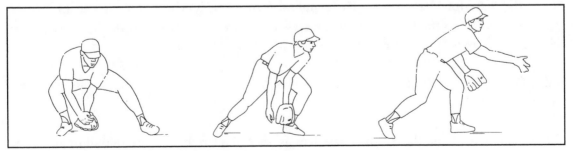

During underhand feeds, flip the ball with a firm elbow.

backhand flip, turn your hand so that the ball is facing the target and the fingers are facing the outfield. Your arm will have begun in a bent position. The action of the flip is completed by straightening out the arm towards the target. Visually, the backhand flip looks similar to a police officer sticking out his arm to stop an oncoming car.

When making any flip toss, forehand or backhand, develop the habit of telling the pivot man. Simply yell "flip" before you make the play. This verbal instruction lets the other player know where the ball will be coming from. On plays near the bag, a "flip" call makes it much easier to be comfortable receiving the ball because you are aware of the release point.

MAC FACT: *Give the double-play partner a verbal cue when you flip the ball underhand.*

The secret to performing all four feeds is, quite simply, practice. You will develop some habits or instincts when working on pivots and feeds. This is acceptable as long as you make the play. Coaches should not get caught up with making sure that every middle infielder performs each feed robotically. Instead, teach the proper mechanics, provide basic skills, and let athleticism take over. Coaching concerns lie with inaccurate throws and, perhaps, slow completion of the task. Once you know how to perform the skill, your objective is practice, practice, and more practice. Every ground ball is different, and you will move and react differently to each one. The more you practice and are confronted with a variety of situations, the more comfortable and prepared you will be on game day.

SECOND BASEMAN FEEDS

Try to keep the feeds as similar as possible for consistent learning. Because you're expected to be able to play both middle-infield positions, it's important to learn all the different feeds. If feeds are taught consistently, then it will be easier to digest. This simplicity can be understood if you realize that all the feeds are the same, except it is like looking in the mirror once you flip over to the other side of the infield. You must feed the shortstop in much the same manner. Again, there are four basic feeds: The standard feed on balls which you can set up to field properly; balls hit in the hole to your left; balls hit between yourself and the base; and short choppers that are hit over the mound.

MAC FACT: *All middle infield feeds should be taught the same way; consistent teaching will help prevent confusion.*

The standard feed for the second baseman is very similar to that of the shortstop. The difference lies in the footwork. At both positions, field the ball by opening your body to second base. If you adhere to the instruction "open up your feet to the base" then you don't have to focus on which foot is forward. The last thing a player wants is to be thinking about her feet when a ball is en route.

At shortstop, the proper footwork is staggering your feet with the right one forward. At second base, on the other hand, you will stagger your feet with the left foot forward. Your feet should be in a heel to toe alignment. Your objective is to open up the lower body to make it easier to feed the pivot man while still trying to keep your shoulders square to the ball.

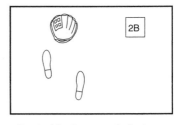

Standard feed: open up to the base.

As you field the ball, pivot on the balls of your feet and drop or lower the left knee to the ground. Throw the ball across your body in a sweeping motion similar to the paintbrush moving sideways. The standard feed is the simplest and most efficient method of getting the ball quickly and accurately to the shortstop. It should be used on any ball that you have time to set up properly.

On balls into the hole between you and the first baseman, initiate movement with a pivot-crossover step and attempt to cut off the ball. Similar to the shortstop, your feed is dependent on which foot is forward when you field the ball. If the throwing-side foot (right) is closest to the ball, pivot on the balls of your feet in the direction which turns your back to home plate, then make a strong, accurate throw to second base. Get your momentum under control before attempting a throw. Try to stay low and avoid popping up to throw the ball.

As you field the ball, drop your right knee and feed the shortstop.

If the glove-side foot (left) is closest to the ball, take a power step back to the base. The power step is initiated by pivoting on the right foot, and turning to the glove side and stepping back to the base. Again, I cannot stress enough the importance of an accurate throw. It will be extremely difficult to complete the double play on any ball hit into the

If your right foot is forward, pivot on the balls of your feet and make a good throw.

If your left foot is forward, try to take a power step back toward the base.

hole, whether it is near the second baseman or shortstop. Make sure of at least one out.

On balls hit between you and second base, flip the ball underhand to the shortstop. The mechanics of the flip are exactly the same as the shortstop. Clear the glove to let the pivot man see the ball. Follow your flip in case of a bad toss. And finally, give a verbal cue to inform the shortstop that the ball will be coming underhand.

If a ball is chopped into the ground and perhaps over the mound, try fielding it on the run. Once you make the play, perform a backhand flip to the shortstop. The ball will be facing the base, with your knuckles pointed towards home plate. The backhand flip is performed by bending the elbow and then straightening out the arm while flipping the ball.

INFIELD DRILLS

#1 — INFIELD SQUARE DRILL

Objective: To practice a lot of ground ball repetitions in a short period of time.
To promote good fielding mechanics.

Setup: You will need four people to hit ground balls and four people to catch. Also, each hitter will need a good supply of balls. All infielders and outfielders should be positioned at the four infield spots. Catchers can also go to an infield position unless needed to catch or hit.

Procedure: The hitters will be stationed directly across the infield from each of the positions. A hitter and catcher will be about one quarter up the foul lines and one quarter of the way before the corner bases. These hitters will hit continuous ground balls to the fielders stationed across from them.

Coach's Note: At the younger levels, try to get other coaches or parents to hit and catch in order to

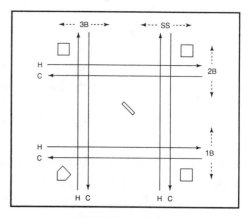

Infield Square Drill.

have more of your players available to field ground balls. At the older levels, you might use pitchers. It is important to observe the mechanics and reinforce good habits. You may want to introduce a reward system for consistent good plays and/or accurate throws. A reward system is effective in maintaining some focus and concentration throughout the drill.

#2 – BLOCKING DRILLS

Objective:　To stress the importance of keeping the ball in front.
　　　　　　　To accustom players to being hit by the ball.

Setup: Have the infielders arrange themselves in pairs. You will need three or four soft touch baseballs for each pair of fielders. Players do not use their gloves.

Procedure: The blocking drills are a two-step process:
1. During the first phase, one player will be on his knees with his hands behind his back. His partner will stand not more than 3 feet away with the balls. Bounce the balls into the chest of the kneeling player while he attempts to form a wall with his body and block the ball while keeping it in front.
2. One player will assume the proper fielding position. Bounce balls off the ground and into the chest of your partner. Your partner is not trying to catch each ball. Rather, she is simply trying to let the ball hit her chest and keep it in front.

Two Step Blocking Drills

Coach's Note: You must demonstrate this drill before letting the players try it. The partner who is bouncing the ball must make good tosses so that the ball hits her partner in the chest, not the face. Force players to get comfortable with the ball hitting them. The goal of any infielder is to be "a wall."

Variation: You can use soft rubber or even tennis balls for this drill. This drill is effective for players who have been clipped in the face by a ball which took a bad hop. It will help that player overcome his fear.

#3 – SCRAMBLE DRILL

Objective: To keep the ball in front.

To react to the ball and complete the play.

Setup: This drill is actually a continuation of the blocking drills. Set it up the same way with partners and soft balls.

Procedure: Start in the proper fielding position while your partner stands a few feet away and bounces the ball into your chest. You are not trying to catch the ball – you want to let the ball hit you and become comfortable with that feeling. Once the ball bounces off you, react quickly. Approach the ball and set up your feet properly. You must stand directly over the ball with your feet lined up to the target. Pick up the ball with two hands in a scooping motion and bring your hands to your belly button. Initiate the throwing action without actually throwing the baseball.

Scramble Drill

Coach's Note: As with the blocking drills, let each player perform three to five repetitions and then switch. Too many reps will cause the player to get tired and promote bad habits. Stress the importance of setting direction before picking up the ball. Make sure players pick up the ball with both hands. A lot of infielders develop the unfortunate habit of picking up the ball in their bare hand, putting it in the glove, then taking it out again for the throw. Precious seconds may be lost with a fast runner moving down the line.

Variation: With this drill you can begin to incorporate real baseballs, cautiously.

#4 — TWO BALL DRILL

Objective: To promote good hand-eye co-ordination.

Setup: Pair off and stand about 5 feet apart. One player has a ball in each hand. Gloves are not used.

Procedure: Flip both balls to your partner at the same time. The toss should have a slight arc. Your partner will try to catch both balls; one in each hand, and then flip them back.

Coach's Note: The players should start in a good ready position. Make sure that they make good throws to their partner.

Variation: Try a few rounds where each flip is a bounce toss. This drill can be modified so that each partner starts with a ball. They will then throw the ball at the same time that they try to catch the ball coming at them.

#5 — SHORT HOP DRILL

Objective: To field short hops cleanly.
          To work on good fielding mechanics.

Setup: Players are paired off and stand about 30 feet apart. One baseball per pair is needed.

Procedure: As the player without the ball you start in the ready, fielding position. The player with the ball will throw a short hop at you and you then try fielding it cleanly. If it is not fielded cleanly, scramble for the ball and go through the throwing motion.

Coach's Note: Make sure that players are in a good ready and fielding position. The players throwing the ball should vary the speed and spin on the ball. After some time, they can also move the ball slightly to the left and right.

#6 — BALL ROLLS

Objective: To reinforce good fielding mechanics.
To improve quickness.

Setup: Players pair off with two baseballs per group and stand about 6 to 10 feet apart, with or without gloves.

Procedure: As the player with both baseballs, start on your knees and begin by rolling one of the balls to your partner's left about 4 to 8 feet away at moderate speed. Your partner will move to the ball and field it properly and then flip it back. As he flips the ball back, you roll the second ball to the right and your partner moves back the other way. Continue this action until the coach instructs you to switch.

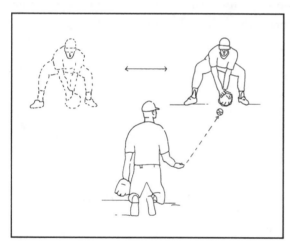

Ball Rolls

Coach's Note: As a coach, see that players concentrate on good fielding position. Of particular concern are the legs. As players get tired, they begin to stand up. This can result in balls being fielded between the legs and not at the top of the triangle. This drill can be used to help condition your athletes. Have them switch on timed intervals of 20 to 40 seconds. Be careful to avoid letting the players continue when fatigue sets in. Tired athletes tend to develop bad habits, thus defeating your desired goal of reinforcing proper mechanics.

#7 — APPROACH DRILL

Objective: To get a feel for the proper approach to the ball.
To reinforce good fielding mechanics.

Setup: Arrange players in pairs about 15 to 20 feet apart. Place a baseball on the ground halfway between them.

Procedure: Charge the stationary ball and set up to field it. Approach the ball as if it were moving and scoop it with two hands to your centre. Set your feet to the throwing position and go through the throwing procedure without releasing the baseball. After simulating a throw, return the ball to its original spot and return to the starting point. Now your partner will go through the same procedure.

Coach's Note: This drill is an excellent warm-up activity. It should not, however, be used for too long, especially with older, more experienced players, who will become bored.

#8 — CONTINUOUS ROLLING DRILL

Objective: To practice many repetitions in a short period of time.

Setup: Group players into two lines with at least two players per line. If more infielders are involved, set up a second group. Position the lines about 30 feet apart. One baseball is required.

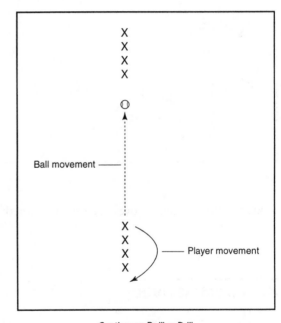

Procedure: The first player in line throws a ground ball across to the first player in the other line, then runs to the back of the line. The fielder will correctly make the play, set his feet, throw a ground ball back across, and then return to the back of his line. Continue fielding and throwing the ball back to the next player.

Continuous Rolling Drill

Coach's Note: This drill can feature players with or without their gloves on. Making the play with no glove is a good method for reinforcing the use of two hands and cradling the ball. Have players vary the speed and spin on their throw to simulate different ground balls.

#9 — GOALIE DRILL

Objective: To stress the importance of knocking the ball down and keeping it in front.

Setup: Arrange players in pairs with one baseball between them. Set up a "goal" area using bats, hats or gloves as the goalposts. The goals should be 10 to 30 feet apart — the width will vary depending on the age group and position. For example, middle infielders may have a goal that is a lot wider than the corner players because they have more ground to cover in a game. Soft touch baseballs or tennis balls are ideal for this drill.

Procedure: Throw the ball back and forth attempting to "score" on your partner. The throws can become more difficult and faster as the drill progresses. "Be a wall" and keep every ball in front of you. If possible, catch it cleanly. If not, at least block it. Keep track of points and set up a reward system for the winning player.

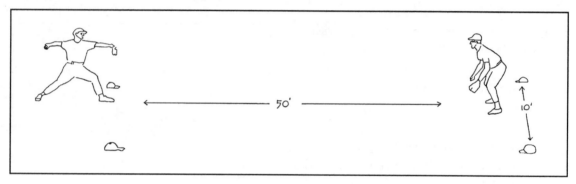

Goalie Drill

Coach's Note: Again, gloves are optional for this drill.

#10 — CROSSOVER DRILL

Objective: To use the proper footwork on balls hit to the left and right.

Setup: Arrange players in a single line one behind another. Do not have too many players per line. If you want more players involved in this drill, set up another drill station. Limit each area to three to five players in order to provide everyone with enough repetitions. A coach will be positioned about 30 feet away with some baseballs.

Procedure: The coach will give a verbal cue for the first player to start. When you hear "go," perform a pivot and crossover step and start running. If you have performed the footwork properly, the coach will throw out a ground ball. Run to the spot where the ball is headed. If possible, turn and square up to field the ball properly. If you do not have enough time, make the play with one hand. Once you have made the play, set your feet and make a good throw to the coach. The coach, in turn, will yell "go" to the next player. After every player has performed the drill in one direction, turn and go the other way.

Coach's Note: Stress the importance of good footwork. If players don't perform good pivots and crossover steps, have them start over. When the fielder is running to the spot, encourage her to face the direction she is running. In other words, discourage players from running sideways with their head and shoulders facing the ball or the coach. This turning of the body slows down the fielder.

Crossover Drill

#11 — PADDLE DRILL

Objective: To reinforce the importance of using two hands.
To develop soft hands.

Setup: Each player needs a wooden paddle. See Receiving Drill #2 on page 37 for instructions on constructing your own paddles. The paddle is worn in place of a glove.

Procedure: Position yourselves in a square about 10 feet apart. Throw the ball around the square as quickly as possible. The ball must be caught before it can be thrown. Add another baseball for excitement.

Coach's Note: Stress the importance of using quick feet and soft hands.

Variation: You may choose to use a soft touch baseball. It isn't necessary to use the square format. You can simply hit or throw ground balls and have players field the ball with the wooden paddle.

#12 — PIVOT SQUARE DRILL

Objective: To practice the pivot at second base.

Setup: Four middle infielders are arranged in a square.

Procedure: The pivot by the shortstop is practiced by throwing the ball around the square in a counter-clockwise direction. Take your left foot to the ball, pop your hips and throw the ball to the player on your right. The next player will receive the ball from the person on his left and complete the pivot. To work on the second baseman's pivot, throw the ball in a clockwise direction around the square. Remember that second basemen will take their right foot to the ball, set the left foot for direction, and then throw the ball to the player on his left. The next player will receive the ball from the player on his right and similarly complete the pivot.

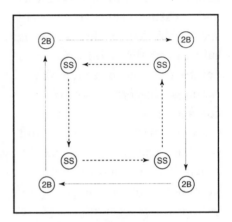

Pivot Square Drill

Coach's Note: Do not use a base for this drill as it may preoccupy the player with concerns about keeping her foot on the base. Instead, let the infielders focus on moving to the ball and using quick feet.

#13 — DIVING DRILL

Objective: To develop confidence and comfort when diving for balls.

Setup: Players are lined up about 20 feet away from the coach on the grass in the outfield. The coach will have a bucket of baseballs.

Procedure: The first player in line starts on her knees. The coach will bounce the ball slightly to her left. She will dive to stop or catch the ball, and quickly get to her feet and throw the ball back to the coach. After four or five attempts, the next player will take a turn. Once each player has practiced diving to her left (glove side), switch it up and throw balls to the other side.

Coach's Note: Players will only get comfortable when they try an activity. By making them dive in this controlled environment, they are more apt to attempt such a play during the game. Starting on the knees will help to eliminate the fear of injury. Preach quick feet to get to the throwing position.

Diving Drill

FOURTH INNING

PLAYING THE OUTFIELD

PLAYING THE OUTFIELD

A common scenario: The team tryout winds down and final player selection is down to thirteen. The coach then decides which position suits each player best, resulting in the most proficient players being assigned the infield, with the weakest roaming the outfield. Yet, in most professional and collegiate programs, top athletes have usually played shortstop, since the position requires an abundance of talent. There are compelling reasons for assuring the presence of talented players in outfield positions, and for training them thoroughly.

Consider the mistake factor. If an infielder makes an error, the result is usually one, or a maximum of two bases. In other words, the batter and base runners can only advance a maximum two bases as a result of an infield miscue. However, if an outfielder makes an error on a fly ball, two bases to the batter and three to any runner are almost guaranteed. Errors in the outfield are considerably more dangerous and increase the number of runs allowed.

As a coach, concern yourself with the amount of practice time dedicated to outfield play. Observe a practice and record the amount of repetitions each outfielder receives, comparing those numbers with the infield repetitions. In most practices, the infield work will outweigh time spent with the outfielders. Often, time spent on outfielders is strictly hitting fly balls to them. In considering outfield repetitions, be sure to devote time to specific drills. Make no assumptions about player expertise. Provide outfielders ample opportunity to build and maintain essential muscle memory. Avoid placing inexperienced players in the outfield and then expecting effective plays.

If you tend to assume that the greatest athletes are in the infield, you may wish to consider some of the testing performed on the Toronto Blue Jays' players. In testing for hand-eye co-ordination, Joe Carter, who patrols the outfield, was discovered to be head and shoulders above all other players on the 1997 roster.

READY POSITION

The ready position for outfielders is equal to the importance of infielders. Because of the dangers presented by misplaying outfield balls, it's imperative that outfielders are prepared for any possibility.

The pre-pitch stance of an outfielder is similar to that of an infielder. You must initiate some motion before the pitch enters the hitting area. Don't forget to "de-cleat" as the ball enters the contact zone. Again, de-cleating means moving the feet in such a manner that the cleats on your shoes leave the ground. This action prevents you from getting caught flat-footed once the ball is in play.

MAC FACT: *The cleats must come out of the ground just before the ball enters the hitting area; get the feet in motion.*

The actual foot movement can be achieved in different ways. Some fielders simply lift their feet off the ground as the ball is being pitched. It appears as if they are walking on the spot. I teach the lower body action of the ready position the same way I teach it to infielders. Consistency in teaching makes more sense when you consider that players at less experienced, younger levels often play both the infield and outfield. In this case, the player will take a creep step as the ball is pitched.

Because you will have to move to the ball as an outfielder, you should be in an upright position. Flex your knees comfortably without extreme crouching. Your feet should be slightly staggered, in an open

Ready position: de-cleat before the ball enters the hitting zone.

position. This positioning is also consistent with proper infield mechanics.

While preparing for the pitch, be sure to face home plate. Standing sideways would limit your reaction time to one side only. Positioning yourself square to the plate enables you to get a good jump on the ball regardless of where it's hit.

MAC FACT: *The goal of the ready position is to place you, the fielder, in a position which maximizes your ability to get a good jump on a batted ball.*

FIELDING FLY BALLS

Although the flair, grace and fancy footwork of pros like Devon White and Ricky Henderson is impressive and invites copying by budding players, it's still most important to stress the proper mechanics of fielding. As a coach at all levels, be emphatic about proper fielding position and using two hands to catch the ball.

Catch the ball on the throwing side of the body. Use two hands and receive the ball above shoulder height, since your hands cannot comfortably drop below the neck line. If your hands do drop, they are forced to turn over with pinky fingers together, perhaps causing you to drop the ball. Also, as the ball passes below eye level, tracking its route to the glove becomes more difficult.

Catch fly balls with two hands above the head.

MAC FACT: *Always catch the ball at or above shoulder height, with two hands, and on thr throwing side of the body.*

Your eyes should track the ball the entire route to the glove. Upon receiving the ball, the hands, wrists, and elbows should give slightly to cushion the impact of the ball hitting your glove. Once the ball makes contact with the glove, your throwing hand will wrap around in front to prevent the ball from popping back out.

Position your hands thumb to thumb facing upwards. Your throwing hand will be slightly behind the glove. If you can't get to the ball in time to set up properly, and are forced to catch the ball below your waist, turn your hands over so that the fingers are pointing down.

FIELDING GROUND BALLS

Three different situations which should be learned by outfielders when dealing with balls hit on the ground: Standard base hits, playing on a rough field, and do-or-die situations. First of all, consider field conditions. Check the playing surface prior to the game, possibly during warm-up. This will help you make decisions about how to handle ground balls.

If the field is rough, drop your throwing-side knee to the ground when fielding the ball. Do this only when there are no runners on base. Position your body in direct line with the ball, keeping your shoulders square. Extend your arms and, using both hands, follow the ball into the glove, cradling it to cushion the effect. Remember, you have to successfully catch the ball before you can throw it!

On a rough surface, drop to one knee to field ground balls.

MAC FACT: *To field a ground ball on a rough playing surface, drop the throwing-side knee.*

When there are runners on base or the playing surface is normal, play ground balls exactly the same way as an infielder. Focus and be consistent. This time, don't drop your knee to the ground. Instead, approach the ball with your glove-side foot slightly ahead (about 2 inches). Distribute your weight on the balls of your feet. Flex your knees so that your upper leg is parallel to the ground. Square up your shoulders, allowing your chest to act as a wall behind the ball. Extend your hands, palm to palm, with the bare hand on top.

MAC FACT: *With runners on base, field a ground ball like an infielder.*

As the ball approaches, follow it to the glove, cradling it into your belly button. From this point, quick feet and hands enable you to change from fielding to throwing position.

With runners on base, field ground balls like an infielder.

After you field the ball, take a positive step to throw.

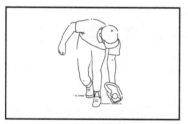

Fielding a ground ball in the "do-or-die" situation.

When a base runner tries for an extra base and the outfielder tries to throw him out, you've found yourself in the middle of a "do-or-die" situation. For example, with a runner on second base, you must charge any ground ball that gets through the infield. The base runner will be trying to score on a base hit. You must stop her.

To throw out a runner, field the ball with your glove-side foot out front. Bend your knees and get the glove snugly down to the ground. Be sure to flex your elbow and drop your head so that you have soft hands. Try to field the ball with one hand, outside of your glove-side foot, then drive the glove and ball to the throwing shoulder to begin the transfer process.

MAC FACT: *When trying to throw out a base runner, field the ball with one hand outside the glove-side foot.*

As the ball is scooped up to the throwing shoulder, perform a "crowhop" to initiate the throwing process (discussed in the next section). This crowhop and scoop will generate good momentum, establish direction, and enable a fast, powerful release of the ball.

THROWING FROM THE OUTFIELD

Always perform a "crowhop" to generate momentum, power and direction for your throw. For right-handed throwers, the crowhop starts the moment you catch the ball. On a ground ball, catch the ball outside your left foot and scoop it to your throwing shoulder, pushing off on your left foot and executing a hop onto your right foot.

MAC FACT: *Do a crowhop by pushing off on your glove-side foot and landing on your throwing-side foot.*

When your right foot (right-handers) lands, it must hit the ground squared to the target. This means you've established proper throwing position. Footwork is reversed for left-handers.

MAC FACT: *When the throwing-side foot lands, it should be square to the target.*

Cover as much distance as possible when working on this skill, as distance is far more important than height. Strive for only enough height to be out in front when you land.

A powerful push-off for the crowhop is crucial. The more drive generated, the more distance covered, and the more momentum is achieved. Momentum results in greater distance

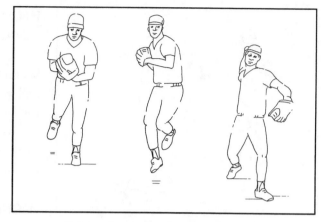

Perform a "crowhop" to throw from the outfield.

on the ball. Like many other movements in baseball, the crowhop is an explosive muscle activity.

MAC FACT: *Push off hard on the throwing-side foot to generate momentum.*

In observing professional outfielders, note their body position after throwing out a runner at the plate. Many of them accumulate so much momentum that their bodies follow right through. Otis Nixon, then of the Toronto Blue Jays, flipped completely over during one game, while trying to throw out a runner. Aware of the limitations of his throwing arm, Nixon made use of the crowhop to assist with momentum.

When working on your crowhop, avoid "skip steps." A skip step occurs when you push off and land on the same foot, usually your throwing-side foot. Skip steps don't come close to generating the same momentum or distance that a good crowhop will. A crowhop will also land you nearer your target, sometimes by as much as a couple of feet. It's important to take advantage of every edge you can think of when the play is on.

MAC FACT: *Avoid using the skip step.*

Outfielder's arm movements will include large circles. You want a generous arc and overhand throw. Releasing the ball overhand keeps the ball from tailing or fading away from the target. The lower the arm slot (i.e. the further the arm gets away from the head), the more the ball tails. This tailing action may cause an otherwise good throw to move several feet off target. More importantly, overhand throws produce a straight skip on bouncing balls. The ball will bounce straight up in the same direction. Low arm slots produce hops which veer left or right of the target, making it tough for the receiver to snag.

Outfielders should use big arm circles when throwing.

MAC FACT: *Use generous, wide arm circles and overhand throws.*

When making a throw, attempt to throw the ball through the head of the cutoff man. The throw should be hard enough to go through to the intended base if desired. Of course, avoid throwing so high that the cutoff man is unable to catch it and make a throw to a different base.

MAC FACT: *Throw the ball so it can be caught by the cutoff man.*

DROP STEP

The drop step is a skill which allows you to get a good jump on balls hit over your head. Make it your first movement as soon as you see the ball set sail.

If the ball is lofting over your right shoulder, pivot on your left foot with toes pointing in. Your right foot will then open up and step straight back so that the toes are pointed towards your target. As the right foot opens up, the upper body will follow. This drop step should position you in good running form to pursue the ball.

Use a drop step on balls hit over your head.

Be certain you really open up on your first step, the drop step. Opening up so that you are then running back is the key to getting a good jump on the ball. Many outfielders take a first step sideways, then not only have to compensate for moving in a direction contrary to the desired goal, but they also have to make additional steps to overcome the first one. A sideways first step loses precious time. A ball falling just out of reach might be caught if the player used a good drop step enabling her to run directly to the ball on first movement.

MAC FACT: *On balls hit over your head, pivot and open up towards the spot where the ball is headed.*

Do the drop step the moment you see that the ball is going to fly over your head. Run with your back to the ball directly to the spot where you judge the ball is headed. For the first few steps, don't watch the ball, just try to get up to full speed, glancing quickly over your shoulder. This requires only a subtle head turn. The shoulders and upper body need not turn to see the ball, since that would slow you down.

MAC FACT: *Run as fast as you can towards the spot where you judge the ball will land.*

Glance over your shoulder to see the ball; do not turn around.

Similarly, perform the drop step for balls hit over your left shoulder. Pivot on your right foot, open up, and drop back with the left foot. Avoid turning to catch the ball unless you have time to set up properly.

Avoid taking a "negative step" back towards the infield when reacting to balls hit overhead. Some players have the habit of taking a first step in the direction of the infield. This first step is considered a negative step because you've then moved in the opposite direction of the ball. This means lost time. Remember that fractions of a second, inches, and a step or two can make the difference between outs, hits, and runs — the difference between winning and losing a ball game.

Whenever you run for the ball, run on the balls of your feet. The pounding effect of running on the heels causes the ball to appear as if it were "bouncing" in the air. Staying on the balls of your feet promotes a softer, clearer line of vision with which to see the ball.

MAC FACT: *Run on the balls of your feet.*

BANANA CURLS

The "banana curl" is a term referring to the pattern you must run to get to any ball, fly or ground, that is not hit directly at you. The approach suggests a banana in that it involves running a small arc to get to the ball. Your arc's depth will vary depending on your position in relation to the ball.

On a ground ball, use either a pivot-crossover step or a drop step in order to get a good first step on the ball. Regardless of the footwork, you will not move directly sideways (at a 90-degree angle), nor will you move straight back. Instead, you should take off on a soft 45-degree angle.

The footwork of a banana curl.

This angle begins your banana arc. If the ball is hit softly, the arc becomes flatter or closer to a straight line. If the ball is hit harder or farther, then make a wider turn, or a larger arc in order to cut down the angle of the travelling ball more effectively. This pattern of running will increase your chances of receiving the ball as it travels toward you, and quickly making the play. Otherwise, you may find yourself running after it, losing precious time, and increasing the possibility of unfortunate errors.

MAC FACT: *Use a banana curl to effectively cut off the baseball and be positioned to make a strong and accurate throw.*

The banana curl allows you to make necessary adjustments to cut off the moving ball. As you approach the ball, you will have made a wide enough turn so that you can approach the ball from behind, which ensures that you're then facing the infield and can more easily set up to make a strong and accurate throw. The proper positioning on a ball hit left or right can compensate for a weak arm. Often, the third-base coach will watch your approach. If he sees you in good position, he probably will not risk his base runner. However, if he notices that you're unable to cut the ball off successfully, he may take more liberties with base runners, forcing you to make an off-balanced throw.

Similarly, on fly balls you can position the body behind the ball and generate momentum to throw out

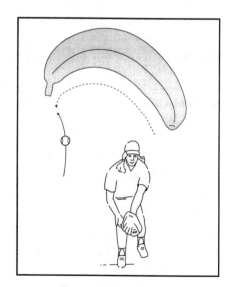

The angle of a banana curl.

any runners. If you're planning a throw to third base, establish a straight line between yourself, the ball, and third base. A banana curl enables you to do that. Remember, direction is essential to throwing mechanics. Good outfielders develop the ability to establish this direction before they make the throw, which saves time.

COMMUNICATION IN THE OUTFIELD

Communicating with other members of the outfield is critical to avoiding injuries and ensuring the ball is caught. If you fail to communicate with your teammates, you risk collisions and the chance of a ball falling into no man's land between you.

There is no one rule, carved in stone, regarding verbal cues used between outfielders. Just use a short, recognizable, verbal sign and be consistent. Common terms include "mine," or "me, me, me," or "I got it." As a coach, encourage all of your fielders to decide what their term will be, and be consistent.

MAC FACT: *Decide on a verbal command which determines who will take charge on a fly ball.*

The outfielder will generally make the final decision on any ball falling between him and the infield. It's easier to come in on a ball than to back up and catch it. Additionally, with runners on base, you're in a better position to make a throw when you're running *in* on the ball. The centre fielder takes a leadership role in the outfield. She assumes control over any accessible ball. In addition, the centre fielder aids the neighbouring fielders on any balls which they must run in on to catch.

As an infielder, pursue any ball hit in the air. But, once the ball is called off by an outfielder, get out of the way. Similarly, the left and right fielders must go hard in pursuit of any ball hit into the gaps until they're called off by the centre fielder. After that they should avoid collision.

FLY BALLS WITH RUNNERS ON BASE

With runners on base, approach every fly ball slightly differently. Treat each play as if the runner will try to advance. Get to where the ball is heading immediately, then set up approximately 3 to 5 feet behind the spot where the ball would land, in an imaginary line between your target base and the ball.

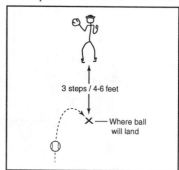

3 steps / 4-6 feet

X — Where ball will land

With runners on base, set up behind a fly ball to get momentum into the throw.

MAC FACT: *With a potential base runner, the outfielder will set up a few steps behind the spot the ball is estimated to land.*

As the ball descends, take the last few steps and catch it at your throwing shoulder, eye level. Receiving the ball in this location makes it easier to transfer the ball from the glove to the throwing hand. As the ball enters the glove, the wrists and arms will cushion the impact and start the transfer process while the ball is coming down.

As the ball descends, start to creep up to the spot where the ball would land. Try to time the catch so that you and the ball arrive together. This timing will start your body moving forward and generate momentum. Use this momentum as you transfer the ball, take a good crowhop, then make a strong throw to the targeted base.

MAC FACT: *As the ball falls, creep in to catch it and use this momentum to explode through the throwing process.*

Your objective is threefold. Cover as much ground as possible with the crowhop. Avoid taking extra steps before releasing the ball. Get rid of the ball as quickly as possible.

Observe the momentum and distance that some professional outfielders achieve while throwing out a runner. Factor in the arm strength of some of those guys and you can witness, and appreciate, some terrific throws from the outfield.

PLAYING THE FENCE

When you arrive at the ballpark, check the fencing. It doesn't matter how old or at what level you play, be aware of the outfield fences. In fact, younger age groups need to be more conscious of the fence because some facilities may not have fencing at all. This is important when dealing with different scenarios in a ball game. For example, is it wise to dive for a ball with two runners on base when you have a three-run lead if there is no fence?

The most compelling reason for checking the fences is to cut down on injuries. Be aware of how the fences are constructed, especially in non-professional parks, whether they are padded or protected in any way, and then proceed accordingly. As a coach,

When you arrive at a park, check the condition of the outfield fence.

make sure that the outfielders are always prepared for the game and know ahead of time what to expect.

Pregame preparation also includes checking for the existence of a warning track. If there is a warning track, become familiar with how it feels beneath your feet. While running, you should be able to feel the difference in surface. The purpose of a warning track is to allow you to know your position while running, with respect to the fence. The track allows you to concentrate on watching the flight of the ball and not worry about running blindly into the fence or wall.

MAC FACT: *Proper pregame preparation is essential to handling balls hit to the fence.*

Once you have a feel for the different surface of the track, determine how many steps you can safely take before running into the wall. Now you can concentrate and focus on the ball, and know your whereabouts in relation to the wall as well.

In addition to proper pregame preparation, two concepts for dealing with the fence should be learned by all outfielders. First, communication is crucial. As outfielders, the three of you must function as a single unit. So communicate with each other on balls hit to the fence. If the right fielder is approaching the fence, the centre fielder must constantly advise him about his distance from the wall.

MAC FACT: *As fielders, advise each other about proximity to the fence when pursuing a fly ball.*

The second concept is to "find the fence first." Use your bare hand to reach behind you and feel for the fence as you are running. Once you've found it, relax in your approach to the ball. Obviously, finding the fence first is only possible on balls that provide you with enough time to go back to the wall and then adjust. If there isn't enough time, then you must rely on a combination of proper pregame preparation and communication.

MAC FACT: *Whenever possible, find the fence first and then adjust to the ball.*

MAC FACT: *Use your bare hand to find the fence, while keeping your eyes on the ball.*

Find the fence with your bare hand while always watching the ball.

In summary, the outfielder should:
- de-cleat on every pitch
- catch the ball with two hands
- field ground balls like an infielder
- catch fly balls on the throwing side
- develop quick feet to get to the throwing position
- use a crowhop to deliver the ball
- use a drop step on balls hit over the head
- employ a banana curl on balls hit left or right
- communicate with and assist fellow fielders
- prepare for the game by observing the surface of the field and location of the fences

OUTFIELD DRILLS

For many of the drills listed here, coaches have several options. Use a regular bat and baseballs when hitting the drills. Or use a pitching machine to deliver the balls to the fielders. A tennis racquet and tennis balls is another alternative.

Using tennis racquets is a very effective option. Young players seem to be enthralled with the cross-referencing of sports. As a result, they find the drill more enjoyable. For the coach, the tennis racket allows you to locate the balls more precisely, so you're using drill time efficiently and not wasting repetitions on uncatchable missiles. Finally, using tennis balls reinforces the importance of playing with both hands. These balls have a tendency to bounce out of the glove, encouraging players to use both hands to trap them.

#1 – QUARTERBACK DRILL

Objective: To teach the proper drop step.

Setup: Find a ball and line up behind the coach. As the first person in line, stand directly in front of the coach, facing him.

Procedure: The coach will take the ball from you, as you maintain an athletic, ready position. When the coach gives the signal you make a good drop step and start running. If you have performed the footwork properly, the coach will throw the ball in the direction that you ran. You attempt to catch the ball and then jog to the back of the line. After each player has attempted a drop step in one direction, do likewise in the other direction.

Coach's Note: Try to throw the ball so the player is forced to make an over the shoulder catch. Make the fielders work hard. Ensure that a simple glance is being used to keep track of the ball, rather than turning the whole upper body

Quarterback Drill

#2 — MISPLAYED BALL DRILL

Objective: To recover on balls that have initially been misplayed.

Setup: Grab a ball and line up behind the coach. As first person in line, stand directly in front of coach and face him.

Procedure: This drill is very similar to the quarterback drill. The difference is the throw by the coach. Instead of throwing the ball in the direction that you made your first step, the ball is thrown over your opposite shoulder once you've glanced for the ball. Upon seeing that you've broken the wrong way on the ball, turn away and cut back to try and retrieve it. Most fielders will try to turn back towards the coach and possibly stumble and fall. By turning away from the ball, you can continue to run hard, then cut back and pick up the ball over the other shoulder.

Coach's Note: The direction of the turn once the player realizes he made a mistake is crucial to this drill. If players have trouble with the footwork, let them try it without a ball.

Misplayed Ball Drill

#3 — DO OR DIE DRILL

Objective: To practice throwing out potential base runners.

Setup: Stand in a single line about 50 feet away from the coach. A cutoff player is needed in addition to the player hitting the ball.

Procedure: Begin in an athletic ready position. The ball is hit directly at you. Charge the ball and field it properly before throwing the ball to the cutoff player.

Coach's Note: Instruct the fielders to be aggressive in getting to the ball. They must charge the ball and use quick feet in order to get rid of the ball quickly. Watch for good footwork and a strong crowhop.

#4 — BANANA CURLS DRILL

Objective: To field balls hit to the left or right.

Setup: Stand in a single line about 20 to 50 feet away from the coach.

Procedure: Start in an athletic ready position. When the coach gives the signal, use a pivot-crossover step. If proper footwork is used, the coach will throw or hit a ground ball or fly ball. You must determine the route and make a banana curl to cut the ball off. After fielding the ball, make a strong throw back to the coach.

Coach's Note: Make sure the player uses effective footwork, as well as a curl that will enable her to be facing her target when it comes time to throw the ball. Vary both ground balls and fly balls depending on your coaching goals for that day.

#5 — COMMUNICATION DRILL

Objective: To develop teamwork in the outfield.
To learn to rely on others.

Setup: You are arranged in two lines, distanced similarly to game setup. One coach is needed.

Procedure: Assume an athletic position. A ball is thrown or hit directly between the two lines. Approach the ball and communicate to determine who will take control and complete the catch. The other fielder will then back up the play and communicate to his teammates.

Coach's Note: Vary ground balls and fly balls to give the fielders practice with both types. Constantly instruct the players to spread the lines further apart as they have a tendency to creep closer together. If you find it helpful, place a glove or hat at the desired starting points. Do not encourage specific outfield positions during this drill. Concentrate on the outfielders' ability to communicate.

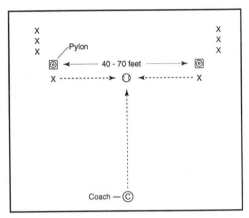

Communication Drill

#6 — TARGET DRILL

Objective: To reinforce the importance of hitting the cutoff man.

Setup: Pair off with one baseball between two players.

Procedure: Use a crowhop to begin each throw. Catch and hold the ball wherever it is caught. If the ball was caught in the head area, you've earned two points. If you catch the ball between the chest and head, award one point. Vary the distance between partners during the drill.

Coach's Note: Since this drill is not time-consuming, it may be implemented during the throwing drills. The purpose is to stress to members of the outfield that they must make a throw which is catchable by a cutoff man.

#7 — TWO BALL DRILL

Objective: To practice running on the balls of your feet.

Setup: Form a single line. Two baseballs are needed by the coach.

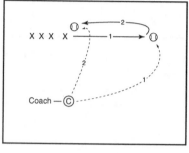

Two Ball Drill

Procedure: Start in an athletic position. The coach will throw or hit the first ball straight up in the air about 20 feet away. You must run on the balls of your feet, set up and catch the ball. As soon as the first ball reaches the highest point of its arc, the second ball is hit or thrown straight up from the original starting position. You must then scramble back and try to catch the second ball. As you're catching the second ball, hold the first ball in your bare hand, without dropping it to the ground where it could trip you up.

Coach's Note: Use this drill to stress the importance of running on the balls of the feet. Remind the players that the ball will appear to bounce if they run on their heels.

#8 — FENCE DRILL

Objective: To create awareness of fence location during the play.
To encourage communication in the outfield.

Setup: Set up with two lines of players about twenty feet apart, facing the coach. The lines are located only 20 feet away from the outfield fence. The coach is positioned about 30 feet in front of the two lines.

Procedure: The first two players in each line will work together. The coach will throw the ball near the fence. You will take control and call for the ball. The other will provide you with verbal assistance. Find the fence first, and then adjust to catch the ball.

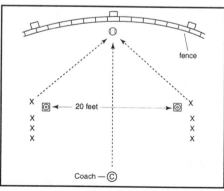

Fence Drill

Coach's Note: Measure the success of this drill by listening to the noise. If the rest of the team cannot hear the outfielders, then their communication skills are lacking. Their voices should be loud and dominant.

#9 — FIELDING DURING BATTING PRACTICE

Objective: To de-cleat on every pitch.
To develop a good first step on balls hit to the outfield.
To acquire some "live" repetitions.

As an outfielder, spend time at your position during batting practice. Do a 10-minute block of "live" repetitions. During this session, treat every pitch as a live situation. De-cleat on the pitch, try to anticipate where the ball is going to be hit, and work on getting a good jump on the ball. This fielding practice is instrumental in developing overall good fielding mechanics. Put all of the skills into practice: drop steps, banana curls, crowhops, do or dies, playing the fence, and communication.

FIFTH INNING
HITTING THE BASEBALL

HITTING THE BASEBALL

Hitting. Mashing. Swinging the stick. Using the lumber. Hitting a seed. Going yard. Hitting a bomb. Losing one. Regardless of the expression, the act of hitting a baseball is the most enjoyable and exciting aspect of the game. It causes fans to leap from their seats, players to race off their benches, and owners to offer more money. Most young players compete in the great game of baseball for those four times in a game when they get to compete one-on-one with the pitcher. Unless he or she is a pitcher, every youngster's favourite position is hitter. But, despite the glory of hitting a game-winning hit to become the hero, the process of developing a quality swing commands a large amount of time and attention.

Hitting a baseball is perhaps the single most difficult task in all of sports. Failing two out of three times in a game is considered a good day. If you can fail consistently at this rate, you can earn a promotion to the next level. Failing at this rate enough times at the major league level will ensure you a spot in the Hall of Fame.

Since hitting the ball is so challenging, different theories and principles for success have evolved over the decades. In baseball's early years, players swung enormous, heavy bats. The pitchers' goal was to try to throw the ball with such speed that hitters couldn't get the bat moving quickly enough to make contact. Pitchers often succeeded. In an effort to gain an advantage, the concept of "weight transfer" hitting developed. Hitters began to "time" the pitcher to figure out how fast they were throwing and plan their swings accordingly. Once hitters developed timing, they were able to transfer weight forward towards the ball and begin to swing. This simple weight transfer meant a faster, more accurate bat.

The game of baseball developed in cycles. Like a game of cat and mouse, once the hitters started making positive adjustments and becoming more successful, the pitchers looked for ways to combat these changes. Hence the development of off-speed pitches. Pitchers began to change the speed of their pitches by throwing curve balls or a straight change. The change of speed made it difficult to time the pitcher, causing hitters to get caught out in front when they transferred their weight and the pitch turned slow. On the other hand, if a hitter was looking for a slower pitch, a good fastball might fly by before she had time to even *think* of swinging. Once again, pitchers gained a dominant advantage.

In order to develop hitters with a chance to effectively hit off-speed pitches as well as fastballs, I teach what is called "backside rotational" hitting. A rotational style of hitting is designed to minimize forward or linear movement, get the hitter in a good position to hit before the ball approaches, and then use the largest group of muscles — hips and legs — to rotate and drive the baseball.

Rotating the hips to hit the baseball is probably the most well-known hitting concept in baseball today. Even though major league players feature many different hitting styles, stances, and approaches to the baseball, hip rotation is an absolute necessity in all swings.

BAT SELECTION

Choice of a bat is a key ingredient to successful hitting at the youth, or inexperienced level. Young players often seek out the biggest, heaviest bat in the rack. Then they wonder why they can't make solid contact with the ball. Since young players are often of a determined nature, they may develop some habit, or resort to cheating, in order to make that contact happen. This is often the beginning of a bad habit. As a coach, keep an eye on your players' choice of bat.

To emphasize the wisdom of using smaller and lighter bats, consider these two stories: Tony Gwynn is one of the best hitters ever. He studies every pitcher in the league in order to hone a competitive edge, and wins the batting title almost every year. Gwynn swings a 32 or 33 inch bat, is 5'11" and weighs over 200 pounds. In observing a city all-star team of fifteen year-olds, I noted that at least eighty percent of the players hefted a larger bat than Tony Gwynn. Only one player even came close to Gwynn's physical size and he used a 34 inch, 30 ounce bat! Tony Gwynn knows that a bat's weight increases with length. Although a longer bat would add to his plate coverage, he wisely sacrifices the extra weight and length for speed. Remember too that wooden bats used by pros are heavier than the aluminum ones often used by amateurs.

The second story regarding bat selection concerns legislation being considered by the NCAA (the governing body for the U.S.A. colleges and universities). The maximum difference between length and weight of aluminum bats is five points. In other words, if the bat is 33 inches long, it must weigh at least 28 ounces. About ten years ago, most bat companies routinely produced bats with a three-point differential. The length/weight ratio then became four points. The manufacturers learned that college hitters loved having good bat length *and* lightness. These light bats enabled hitters to gain greater bat speed and hit the ball harder.

Studies were conducted to determine reaction time using these lighter bats. It was discovered that because the bats were lighter, and players were able to develop quicker bat speed, the ball would be propelled off the bat faster than it was being thrown. The results were rather terrifying because the speed of the ball leaving the bat was greater than the reaction times of pitchers, increasing their chances of serious injury. Indeed, this is exactly what happened.

When the NCAA studied these results they began to consider changing the bat length to weight ratio. A legal difference of 2.5 points is now under consideration.

MAC FACT: *A lighter bat is speedier and permits a more powerful hit. Bat speed equals power.*

Here are two simple exercises to determine if a bat is too heavy or too long. With one hand, take hold of the bat at its grip and lift it straight out, parallel to the ground. Do the same with the other hand. If you can lift the bat with relative ease, it's an appropriate weight. To test for proper length, place a batting tee on the inside corner of home plate and hit it using your regular swing from the correct position. If you can't hit the tee with the barrel of the bat, it's too long.

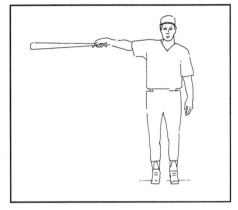

Test to determine if the bat is too heavy.

In general, high school players should avoid using bats weighing more than 28 or 29 ounces, especially with the availability of ultralight bats. Listen to the message the best amateur players (who will be the next crop of professionals) and the bat manufacturers are sending.

THE GRIP

The bat is gripped in three possible ways: Deep in the palms; on the pads just below the root of each finger (callous area); and on the fingers themselves. Each grip has its own advantages. Here are some guidelines to determine the best grip:

Step one: Open your left hand wide. Place your right forefinger in the base of your hand, so that it points at your thumb. Now, close your left hand over the finger and squeeze as hard as you can. Try to pull your right forefinger out of that grip.

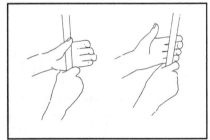

A weak grip (left) provides poor flexibiltiy; a strong grip (right) — gripping the bat with the fingers — provides good flexibility.

Step two: Using the same sequence, place your right forefinger in the area where your fingers start, between the knuckles and pads of the hand. Now, try the same thing. Which grip is stronger? Invariably, the answer will be "gripping it in the fingers."

Using a grip where the bat's handle is tucked into your fingers provides more power than when the handle is tucked into the palm. This strong grip is important when you're trying to swing a weighted object at maximum speed. Gripping the bat out in the fingers also allows more wrist flexibility. Choking the bat deep in your palms restricts wrist flexibility, preventing you from achieving maximum range of motion and top bat speed. Remember: *Bat speed is power.*

MAC FACT: *Grip the bat in your fingers for greater strength and flexibility!*

When you grip the bat out in your fingers you should notice an alignment of your knuckles. The knuckles in the middle of your fingers of the top hand will line up between the two sets of knuckles on your bottom hand. Looking for this alignment is a convenient self-check before entering the hitting area.

Ensure proper alignment of the knuckles.

THE STANCE

Now that you've properly selected a bat and know how to hold it, you're ready for the batter's box. One of the key components of a good hitting stance is comfort. You must be comfortable. MOST CHANGES WILL NOT BE COMFORTABLE. Let me repeat that caution in different words. ANY NEW CHANGE WILL PROBABLY CAUSE IMMEDIATE DISCOMFORT. This word of caution is important because many players resist or are impatient with adjustments simply because they "feel weird." The discomfort associated with changes is only short-term. Eventually, you'll get used to a new feeling or experience, especially if it's beneficial.

Everyone's hitting stance is unique, as a quick look at the major leagues proves. However, avoid copying some of the extreme stances. Some of the outrageous hitting stances featured by major leaguers are the result of a hitting flaw. In order to overcome that flaw, the player will modify an earlier part of the hitting stage. In other words, an extreme stance is often used to force a hitter to get in a good hitting or "load" position (discussed at length later).

Your first challenge is to get comfortable. Regardless of how this state of comfort is achieved, feel relaxed and loose while waiting for the pitch.

Approach a good hitting stance from the bottom up. Your weight should be on the balls of your feet and evenly distributed between both legs with your feet shoulder-width apart. The knees should be flexed. This is the point where a lot of players differ. My theory relates back to that of comfort. Flex those knees to a point of comfort. If you feel better bending down lower (like Rickey Henderson) then do so. It may even help you see the ball better. If you prefer standing up straight, then go right ahead. Again, the key is comfort.

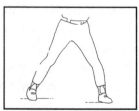

Lower body stance.

Your toes should point straight ahead. Some instructors prefer a pigeon-toed approach, which is fine as long as the player is comfortable. At this point, every hitter, regardless of the differences in stance, should be in a good ready position.

Your stance becomes more complex as you move to the upper body. Your hands should be holding the bat a few inches away from the back shoulder. In this position, your hands will be at the back side of your body, away from the pitcher, and at shoulder height. Elbows should be loose and relaxed.

One of the most common hitting fallacies is "keep your back elbow up." This teaching is problematic because as you begin your swing, your elbow heads downward naturally. With the back elbow up, the barrel of the bat moves away from the ball, the opposite of what you want as a hitter. As well, if your bat is moving away from the ball initially, it isn't moving quickly to the hitting zone. A high back elbow causes a slow bat, which decreases power in your swing. Finally, keeping the back elbow up is uncomfortable and unnatural — very likely a muscle memory which has developed into a bad habit.

Upper body stance.

MAC FACT: *Ignore the back-elbow-up teaching!*

When getting into batting position, remember "point the knob of your bat at the opposite batters box." This is a valuable point of reference which helps to make up for the fact that you can't see your own stance. You can perform a little self-check to see if your bat is in a good position by simply checking the knob of the bat. This will result in a good, 45-degree bat angle. From this position, your bat can take a direct and quick route to the pitch. If your bat is straight up and down, it must first loop before approaching the ball, reducing bat speed.

You can initiate your stance with the bat leaning on your shoulder. This is an excellent starting point because it places your hands in an ideal location with proper bat angle. The rule "get your bat off your shoulder" is directed at the hitting stage, not the preliminary stance. While it isn't necessary to begin with the bat on your shoulder, it's one method of correcting a stance with a poor starting point. Also, it ensures that you don't wrap the bat around the back of your head, which causes a long and slow swing.

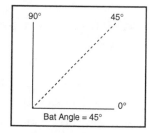

Proper angle of the bat.

Follow these cues for proper hitting stance:

- weight on the balls of the feet
- weight evenly distributed on both feet
- feet shoulder-width apart
- knees flexed

- hands at back shoulder, and shoulder height
- elbows relaxed
- bat at a good angle
- do not wrap the bat
- be comfortable and relaxed

THE STRIDE

Your stride is the first move you make toward hitting. Your stride places you in the best position to hit the ball. The stride is not designed to enable you to hit the ball. Rather, it puts you in a desirable ready position prior to hitting the ball. This position is the "load phase" of hitting and will be discussed later.

Not only is your stride a pre-hitting, preparatory movement, it is also somewhat contradictory. The action itself involves a short movement of your front foot towards the pitcher. At the same time, you shift your weight to the back foot. The twofold action involves movement in opposite directions.

When learning the stride phase of hitting, start again by separating the upper and lower body. Your front foot begins the process by taking a very short (2 to 6 inches long) step towards the pitcher. I describe this step as a "toe tap." Move the front foot easily, quietly, and lightly. The heel of this foot should be off the ground, and your knees flexed. Point your toes in the same direction as they started during the stance. Don't open up your front foot by pointing it at the pitcher, as this will reduce your power and plate coverage.

At the same time, shift your weight to your back leg. As a coach, observing the "toe tap" with the player's heel off the ground will help ensure that her weight has in fact been shifted to the back side. If her front foot heel clears the ground, then chances are greater that this weight shift occurred.

MAC FACT: *Take a short, light, soft stride towards the pitcher while shifting your weight to the back leg.*

You can practice this with hands on hips. While you're practising, the coach can test to see if the proper weight shift occurred by trying to lift your back leg. If the coach can move your back leg easily, then not enough weight has been shifted to the back side. If your back legs feels strong and firm, then good weight transfer resulted. Practice this movement by concentrating strictly on the lower body first before considering the upper body and the bat. Doing repetitions in front of a mirror is extremely helpful to ensure a good stride.

Your upper body also serves a function during your stride. It's important that your head and eyes remain on a level plane, focused on the the ball. Head movement, up or down, during the stride, or during any part of the hitting process, can cause severe problems.

MAC FACT: *Avoid up or down movement with the head and eyes during the stride.*

The role of your hands during your stride varies with the hitter. If you begin with the bat on your shoulder, your hands will make a slight movement during the stride to lift the bat off the shoulder and the hands a few inches away from the body. If your hands are positioned above your ear (like Juan Gonzalez), then they should move down to the back shoulder, to shoulder height. During the stride phase, your hands must achieve that optimum point at the back shoulder, at shoulder height, regardless of the starting point. This hand movement provides good momentum when you start your swing. Remember that the knob of the bat should still be pointed at the opposite batter's box in order to ensure good bat angle and to prevent you from wrapping the bat around your head. Start your hands moving prior to the swing.

A good, balanced stride.

You may wonder at what point during a pitcher's delivery you should initiate your stride. The answer will vary from hitter to hitter depending on where your eyes are focused. Generally, begin the stride as the pitcher's arm accelerates towards you. Remember, the stride is a pre-hitting movement, so begin and complete this action before you swing the bat. To emphasize this point, try swinging a bat with your front foot in the air and you'll see that the front foot must be on the ground before you can swing, and the stride action must be complete.

MAC FACT: *Start your stride as the pitcher's arm moves forward.*

What happens if you stride too late? We know that you cannot swing the bat with your front foot in the air— you must complete the stride by getting your front foot to "toe tap" before you can swing. But, if you have to wait for the foot to land in order to swing, the ball is upon you. The result might be a pitch on the handle of the bat, or no contact at all. It would appear that you have a slow bat, but an earlier stride would have begun the swing earlier and increased your chances of making contact.

If you take a stride too early, don't stride again, as this often results in a late stride. Once that front foot lands, leave it there.

MAC FACT: *Take one stride only!*

If you have taken your stride too early, the only necessary precaution is to make sure that your weight has been effectively shifted to your back side. As long as your weight is back and your front foot down, you're in a position to swing the bat. The problem that usually occurs with an early stride is an impatient lunge at the ball. As long as you "stay back," an early stride is no different than hitting off-speed pitches. You just have to wait longer to initiate your swing.

Stride early with the front foot and leave it there. A late stride will result in little or no contact, while an early stride can still result in a hard-hit ball, if you remember to keep your weight back.

As a strategy, beginning the stride early can be useful in situations where careful batting discipline is in order; it forces you to stay back and try for a hard focused hit, rather than trying for the fence. Consider this when you may be in a slump, or have two strikes against you.

Timing of the stride affects how players and coaches should deal with an opposing pitcher who throws very hard. Inevitably, batters appear to be slow or behind when facing good fastball pitchers. The best adjustment would be to stride earlier which gives you a quicker bat.

At one point, the no-stride theory of hitting gained some popularity, although no major league hitter uses such a style. The closest player, the one that no-stride theorists appeal to, is Paul Molitor. Yet Molitor does use a short, soft and quick stride. One of the most perfect, textbook swings in the league belongs to him, and his stride is well worth emulating. The no-stride concept can be useful during hitting drills, as it helps ensure good weight transfer. However, I wouldn't suggest it as an approach to hitting.

Your stride generates movement and momentum in preparation for the hit. As an example, imagine two cars of equal speed at a drag race. They won't race head to head but will be timed, the clock beginning once they hit the start line. The first car starts right on the line. When the accelerator is pushed the time clock begins. The second car starts one-half mile before the start line, so when it reached the starting line, and the start of the clock, it was already approaching 100 mph. Which car would win? Obviously, the car with the running head start would be victorious. This analogy serves to demonstrate the advantage and purpose of your stride. By getting the bat moving early, and gaining momentum, your bat will be quicker, and therefore more powerful when it makes contact with the ball.

In summary, absolutes of a good stride include:
- keeping the weight and hands back
- being short, soft, on the balls of your feet
- starting your stride when the pitcher's arm is moving forward
- employing slight hand and bat movement to generate momentum
- not wrapping the bat
- keeping the head level
- toes pointing in the same direction as in stance

THE LOAD POSITION

The load position is not an active hitting movement, but another pre-hitting goal or objective. The load position gives you the most effective posture as the pitcher releases the ball, so that you can make solid contact with the ball.

At the load position, your weight will be back and the hands properly located with slight movement in order to develop momentum. If you have a tendency to drop your hands when you stride, then you haven't placed yourself in the best position to swing. You would have to catch up to the ball in a very short time. Don't opt for hand movement if it compromises the goal of getting to a proper load position.

MAC FACT: *No hand movement is better than too much, or poor movement of the hands.*

If your stance features the bat resting on your shoulder, then the hand movement to get to the load position is as simple as taking the bat off your shoulder. If your hands began slightly away from the body, then draw small circles with the knob of the bat. Ideally, these circles will be the size of a baseball and occur at your back shoulder without dropping below shoulder height.

Avoid wrapping the bat behind your head.

Finally, your hand movement should be initiated by the top hand. If your bottom hand starts the action, the bat often becomes wrapped around your head. By starting the hand movement with the top hand, however, the entire bat will move, which is the objective — to get the bat started.

As we move up in age bracket and skill level, another dimension can be added to the load position or pre-hitting phase. This is a concept called "inward rotation." Slightly turn your front shoulder in towards the plate. Remember the direction of your toes as your front foot completes a soft stride — facing forward and avoiding opening up towards the pitcher. Inward rotation helps to keep you in a "closed" position. Closed implies that the hips, shoulder, and feet have not started to open up to the pitcher. Once you start to open up, especially your hips, then you lose power. Stay closed until it is time to explode the hips.

Good hand movement should cause a slight inward turn of the front shoulder which will keep you closed until it is time to swing.

The best way to practice inward rotation is to use a mirror. Watch yourself in a mirror and check to see that your body doesn't open up too soon. You'll find that good inward rotation also creates good hand movement. The two movements complement each other. Wait until the player has developed a solid hitting foundation before introducing some of these refinements.

In summary, the load position:
- is the optimum posture at the end of the stride phase
- is in constant movement
- places the hitter in a "ready" position to hit the ball
- will feature inward rotation and hand movement at the higher levels

THE PIVOT

Pivoting, which is vital to the hitting phase, is lacking in many player's swings. The pivot is a lower body move, allowing the hips and legs, the largest muscle group in the body, to begin the swing, generate bat speed, and transfer power through the bat to the baseball.

The pivot
(front view).

To complete the pivot, turn your back knee in and rotate, or pivot, on the ball of your back foot so that your hips turn and rotate. When the pivot is completed properly, your laces, knees, and belly button will all be facing the pitcher. Your weight should shift back to the middle of your body.

Three terms might clarify the back foot pivot. The first is Drop'n Lock: The front heel begins off the ground in the load position. When you opt to swing, you will drop your heel to the ground, firming up your leg by locking the knee and the entire front side. Locking out the front side assists in the rotation of the hips while ensuring that your weight stays back.

The second term when teaching the pivot is Squish the Fly: If you were asked to squish a fly, you would start twisting on the ball of your foot to grind it into the dirt. This action is a pivot.

Third, you want your Heel to the Sky: When your back foot pivots, lift your heel and use the ball of your foot.

MAC FACT: *Complete the pivot by squishing the fly and keeping your heel to the sky.*

Your weight should rest on the balls of your feet with the heel of the front foot flat on the ground. Your back heel should

The pivot (side view).

be off the ground. Your front leg will be straight and locked. Your back leg will be bent in the shape of an "L." Your head will be balanced in the centre of your body.

Weight transfer during the pivot is significant to the hitting process. At the load position, your weight is back (about 75 percent on the back leg). As you pivot, your weight will shift to the middle so that it is again evenly distributed, like it was in your starting position or stance.

MAC FACT: *Your weight shifts from the back to the middle during the pivot.*

It's important that your head remain balanced and still during the entire swing process. If your head moves too far forward, you may shift your weight forward too, which will drain power from your swing. If you move your head towards the ball, it may be at the rate of three to five miles per hour. Because your head is moving towards an object coming toward you, the pitch will arrive even faster. In other words, an 80 mph fastball is now around 84 mph. You've been a good assistant to the pitcher without meaning to be. You might ask yourself why, for instance, a golfer doesn't take a running start before taking a swing at the ball. Obviously all that movement decreases accuracy in golf. It does the same in baseball.

The backside pivot involves your whole body in the hitting motion. If you forget to turn your back foot (i.e. pivot) then your hips can't rotate and the large leg muscles aren't involved in the swing. This means you're using only your arms to swing, decreasing the power.

MAC FACT: *A greater hip explosion during the pivot means quicker bat speed and more power!*

A proper pivot is the foundation of a great swing. Master the stance, stride, and pivot, focusing strictly on the lower body before proceeding to the upper body portion of swing mechanics.

MAC FACT: *Teach the lower body first — stance, stride, and pivot.*

The pivot, the key to any hitter's swing, will feature:
- drop'n lock
- squish the fly
- heel to the sky
- good quick hip rotation
- laces and belly button finishing by facing the pitcher
- a locked front side
- weight shift from back to middle
- an "L" shape in the back leg
- limited head movement

THE UPPER BODY SWING

Once you have a good grasp on a comfortable stance, a good stride, and a strong back side pivot, then begin to establish the desired swing path, or route of the bat to the baseball.

During the stance, the bat is at an angle and somewhat upright. Get your bat on a level plane, the same as the ball, as quickly as possible. For speed, the bat must take the straightest route to the contact zone.

The contact zone is the area in which you are able to make contact between bat and ball. Some hitters have a larger contact zone. The larger this zone, the better opportunity you have to make consistent contact.

Take the barrel, the fat part of the bat, straight to the ball. During your bat's path to the ball, make sure your hands are always above the ball until it hits the bat. Your hands will be in between your body and the ball. The bat should take a short, quick route to the contact zone, followed by a long, level path following through the zone. In other words, quickly get to the area where contact can be made and stay in that area. Do not let the bat loop. Go straight to the ball. Keep the barrel of the bat above the hands during the swing. When the barrel drops, your bat's surface area is diminished so the ball is more likely to foul off that smaller piece of it.

MAC FACT: *Be short and quick to the contact zone; and long through the zone!*

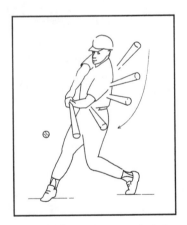

Take a short, quick route to the ball.

Your objective is to hit line drives and hard ground balls. When a ball is hit hard on the ground, the fielder must move to the ball, pick it up, throw to first, and hope for a good catch by the first baseman. Four actions are required to throw out a hitter who puts the ball in play on the ground, so your chances of taking the advantage have doubled that of a flyball, where movement to the ball and a catch are all that is required for the out.

Often, the breathtaking feats of major league hitters puts a low priority on hitting balls on the ground. When Little Johnny or Julia see a ball hit 450 feet by an uppercut swing, they naturally want to copy. Although major league hitters know that the ability to drive home spectacular runs increases their pay cheques, they would readily admit that swinging up on the ball and trying for the fences reduces their batting average considerably.

When I found myself facing Dwight Gooden in 1985, I'd been struggling since opening day. I'd had plenty of batting practice and knew all about "swinging down" on the ball. For some reason, I decided to swing down on any pitch he threw. When he threw me his best fastball and I tomahawked it, really chopped down, the noise was like a gunshot but the feel was weightless. When I looked up the ball was about 450 feet away and still moving. I wasn't fouling off pitches with an uppercut anymore. I won my third MVP.

— Mike Schmidt, The Mike Schmidt Study

To encourage line drives and ground balls, think about the phrase, "swing the bat like an axe chopping a tree." You wouldn't try to chop a tree down with an uppercut or lifting action. You take the axe the shortest and quickest route to the tree, in a downward angle from above your shoulder to the point of contact.

MAC FACT: *When you swing your bat, remind yourself how to chop down a tree.*

The pivot begins the swing. Using the pivot as a starting point ensures that a good back side pivot will occur on every swing. If you don't pivot, don't swing the bat. Secondly, the pivot starting point allows you time to cancel your swing if the ball arrives outside the strike zone. Your hips will start to explode and you may not be able to check them, but because the hands start shortly after, you might be able to check your swing by stopping the hands. It isn't unusual to see a player check his upper body swing while still completing a full pivot. No problem here. In fact, checking your hands while still committing your hips is an effective way to lay off curve balls that drop out of the strike zone. Lastly, the pivot begins the swing because it means getting the larger muscle group started first and transferring the generated power to the hands and bat. The start of the pivot should trigger the hands to start the swing movement. The time in between the two movements is brief, but it's the pivot that gets the bat started.

Key elements of the upper body portion of the swing include:
- first developing a good lower body base
- the bat taking a good route; moving the hands inside to the ball; taking the barrel of the bat straight to the ball
- always keeping the barrel of the bat above the hands
- moving short and quick to the contact zone; moving long through the zone
- hitting the ball hard and on the ground
- not letting the bat loop
- pivoting to start the swing

THE POINT OF CONTACT

Where you make contact with the baseball will depend on the location of the pitch. On an inside pitch, contact will be made out in front of the plate. Be very quick to get the barrel of the bat through the zone and out in front so that the fullest part of the bat meets the ball squarely. Because contact is made out in front, inside pitches are pulled. This explains why most hitters have more power to their pull side (left field for right-handed hitters): they get the barrel of the bat on the ball after it has gained a lot of speed. A slow bat on inside pitches results in a weak hit as the ball makes contact with the handle of the bat. This is referred to as "getting jammed." Getting jammed by inside fastballs creates sore hands, a poorly hit ball, and a pitcher strutting around the mound, proud of his recent success.

When a ball is hit up the middle, your bat should be square to the pitcher. A ball that is pulled will feature a bat angle that has the barrel out in front of the hands. A ball hit up the middle will not have such an angle, as the hands and barrel will be even when contact is made.

Pitches on the outside part of the plate should be hit the opposite way. Contact is made deeper in your body, usually just inside the back foot. In other words, let the ball enter further into the hitting area before making contact. Hitting the ball the other way involves a bat angle where the hands are out in front of the barrel of the bat. Nonetheless, you still should have accomplished your goal of getting the thickest part of the bat on the ball.

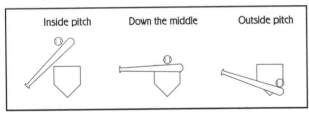

Inside pitch   Down the middle   Outside pitch

The different points of contact.

To be sure about the correct point of contact for different pitches, follow the old baseball adage of hitting the ball where it is pitched. Pull inside pitches, return balls over the middle back up the middle, and go the other way with balls thrown away.

MAC FACT: *Hit the ball where it is pitched!*

Try to get the barrel of the bat out in front of certain pitches so that you can drive the ball. The key, however, is recognizing certain pitch locations, especially pitches over the middle to the inner half of the plate.

Your top arm is the arm of strength and should be bent, regardless of where contact is made between the bat and ball. Your bottom arm is responsible for the direction of the bat and will be straight. Considerable debate has raged over whether the top arm should be bent or straight at contact. Think about pushing a car out of the snow (or sand if you live in a sunny climate!). When trying to push the car out, will your arms be bent or straight? They are always bent because this allows you to use more strength. Similarly, when hitting a baseball, place yourself in a position of strength by having the top arm bent on contact. You probably won't notice if your top arm is bent or not at the exact point of contact, nor should you be thinking about this while trying to smack an 80 mph fastball. However, being aware of the contact point helps you to think about getting to a position of essential strength.

Problems occur when you try to make contact too far out in front of the body. Because of the angle of the bat, you've limited the amount of field. If you're a right-handed hitter, then you can only hit the ball in the area between the left centre alley and the left field foul line. Vice versa for left-handed hitters. But, what happens if you start your swing a bit early? Then you've hit the ball foul, or you get caught leaning out in front because your bat is at the contact point before the ball has arrived. There is very little room for error. As a result, a hitting pattern of strikeouts with occasional long blasts develops.

Your top hand is bent at contact to maximize your strength.

The second problem with trying to make contact out in front on every pitch is your vulnerability to off-speed pitches. When you make contact in front of the plate, you must start your swing earlier, and so you have less time to pick up the rotation and location of off-speed pitches. The result is often swinging at curve balls in the dirt.

The third problem involves using your physical strength. A player is stronger in a shorter, more compact area. Once your bat gets too far away, and your arms straighten out, you lose strength and power. Conduct an experiment to discover the extent of your power. Extend the bat to an imagined contact

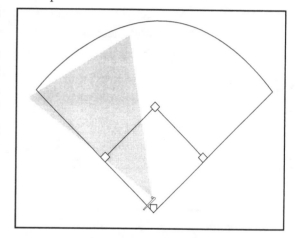

When you try to pull every pitch, you have very little area to get a hit.

point out in front so that your arms are straight. Hold the bat in that position as firmly as you can. Have someone attempt to push the bat backwards. Then extend the bat to an imagined contact point but keep your top arm bent. This contact point can still be out in front, but not as far as in the first step of the experiment. Once again, have someone attempt to push the bat backwards while you put up as much physical resistance as possible. The time when you felt stronger and better able to resist will be the second scenario. Bending the top arm, and not allowing the bat to extend too far at contact, is most effective.

Good extension is essential to the swing. This extension should occur just after contact.

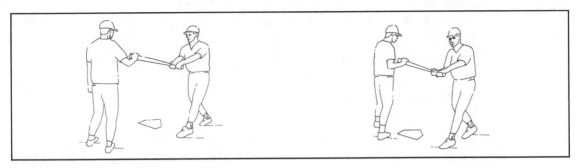

Notice how your strength diminishes if your bat gets too far out in front at contact.

By making contact deeper, you are using more of your physical strength.

THE FOLLOW-THROUGH

The swing is not finished just because you hit the ball. Finish your swing and take the bat the entire route. A complete follow-through features good bat extension through the ball. Allow your wrists to roll over and the bat to continue in a route to the back and side of your shoulder.

The bat should finish at the point of your shoulder, level across your back.

Take the bat the entire route to ensure maximum bat speed at contact. This route starts at your back shoulder and finishes at the back side of your front shoulder. If the bat stops on contact, then you've started slowing it down prior to contact. This action directly contradicts your hitting goal.

MAC FACT: *Take the bat the entire route — shoulder to shoulder.*

The bat should finish at the side of your shoulder, not on top, ensuring a level swing. If your bat ends up on top of your shoulder, you may have used an uppercut or lift in your swing. Finishing too high means that you would have to begin lifting the bat out of the zone earlier, preventing solid contact on the ball, which then goes foul or is an easy pop up. Don't forget that you're hitting a round ball with a round bat. A slight variance in the swing changes the direction of a batted ball. If you finish too high, you've lifted the bat too early, perhaps by only a fraction of a second. In this fraction of a second, the bat could have moved a half-inch, affecting the amount of surface area available for contact between the bat and ball.

Another follow-through checkpoint is the angle of the bat when it is finished the swing. If the bat is level when you complete the follow-through, then it would have been level during the swing. If the bat is angled so that the barrel is lower down your back, then your bat route was probably poor.

A two-handed follow-through ensures a complete swing, but there is nothing wrong with removing the top hand from the bat, as long as it's been swung hard the entire way. Remember that if you remove your hand too soon, you cheat yourself of some power. Make sure that top hand stays on the bat until the bat reaches your front shoulder. It is quite feasible that good bat extension combined with bat speed and momentum will force the top hand off once the bat gets to the front shoulder. Such a finish is acceptable.

For a good follow-through, observe these rules:
- bat extension occurs after contact
- take the bat the entire route
- the barrel should finish level at the back of the front shoulder
- the handle will hit the side and not the top of the shoulder
- do not slow the bat down

OVERVIEW

Hitting is one of the most difficult skills in all of sports. To master it requires hard work, effort, and dedication. As a coach or player your goal is to develop and reinforce a good swing. Once you achieve a good fundamental hitting base, commit it to your "muscle memory." When your swing is automatic, your muscles will know exactly how to perform that skill all the time. Use a hitting partner, coach, or mirror to assist you. Conduct self-checks to make sure you're reinforcing the correct movements. Whether or not your partner understands all of the terms involved in your routine, she can still watch and see if you're "squishing the fly."

Competition isn't the best place to develop muscle memory. Practice the fundamentals of your swing. Take ten or twenty or a hundred swings a day so that your swing is consistent. On game day, when you step into the box, you can concentrate solely on watching the ball. You're at an obvious disadvantage if you step into the box wondering about the angle of your bat, keeping your "heel to the sky," or finishing your swing. Accomplish these mechanical skills through practice and repetition beforehand. You can practice the mechanics of your swing anywhere, anytime, without even using a bat or a ball.

Maintain a consistent swing during the game itself. Don't change it because your first two swings turned into strikes. Be more cautious without moving up in the box or choking up on the bat. Your focus, with two strikes, should be making sure you're short and quick to the ball. Make mental adjustments, but avoid making physical adjustments to your swing during the course of competition.

One final message on hitting. With the exception of pitchers, most young athletes play baseball because they enjoy hitting. It's your job as a coach or player to make hitting a priority. Swinging the bat most often results in failure. And if you do not improve your rate of failure, you may not continue to play the game. As a coach, offer enough instruction and practice time so that players can improve, stay in the game, and enjoy it over the years.

THE STANCE	THE STRIDE	THE PIVOT
THE SWING	CONTACT POINTS	THE FINISH

HITTING DRILLS

These are drills designed to assist you with the development of an efficient batting swing. Properly practiced they will reinforce existing hitting skills, promote positive muscle memory, and eliminate any negative hitting faults or habits.

Three terms must be introduced and understood: Dry swings; batting tee; and soft toss.

A dry swing means going through the batting motions with no actual ball. Swing for the simple purpose of concentrating on the mechanics involved.

Most players at the major league level are advocates of using the batting tee to work on their swing. You can move the tee to any location, thus allowing hitters to work on specific pitch locations and heights.

Unless the drill requires it, don't place the tee too far in front of the body. The tee should be located within the distance established by your feet. The distance between your feet offers enough mobility for work on different pitch locations. When the tee is placed too far in front of the body, you must lunge in order to make contact, resulting in poor hitting mechanics.

However, by all means, move the tee around. The tee should be moved up and down, as well as in and out to simulate different pitch locations over the plate during an actual game. Keep the tee within the distance established by the width of your feet.

Whereas a dry swing involves no object whatsoever, and the batting tee features a stationary ball, soft toss involves hitting a moving object. Standard soft toss includes a partner — the tosser — located to the side of the hitter about four feet away on the far side of the opposing batter's box. The tosser will loft the ball lazily into the hitting zone. The ideal loft would reach a peak height around your waist and not drop below knee level until after the hitting zone.

The tosser plays an important role in soft toss drills. As a coach, spend time teaching players how to be an effective feeder for soft toss drills. Good consistent feeds are essential so that players can work on swings without developing bad habits due to poor tosses.

Work in pairs, especially since many of the drills require a partner to feed the tee or soft toss. Take five swings and

Using a batting tee.

Soft Toss Drills

then rotate. A set of five swings would be more than any at-bat during a game, so it doesn't make sense to take ten or twenty swings at one time. Similar precautions should be taken during batting practice. You do not have to limit the number of rounds or sets, but the number of repetitions should be counted. Keep in mind the bat has some weight. Every time an action is performed with a weight, your body reacts. Eventually, your body's reaction will slow down due to fatigue. Tired players tend to lose their focus and allow bad habits to develop. Keep fresh by taking quick rounds. As you become tired, your bat speed will drop. Since bat speed is a quality you want to improve, don't let practice habits contradict those intentions.

Whenever a partner is used in a drill, thoroughly involve them. Learning is greatly enhanced by teaching others, even more so than by listening. The feeder should be an active participant in the drill by giving verbal commands and offering feedback to you, the hitter. First, he or she will make sure that your stance is good and offer feedback. When your stance is good, he or she can give a verbal command to start the hitting process by telling you to take your stride. Only if your stride is correct will the feeder instruct you to swing or pivot. The feeder plays an important role in assisting you to separate your stride from the swing. You, on the other hand, should respond to the verbal commands of your partner and should ask for feedback.

#1 — MIRROR DRILL

Objective: To observe your own hitting stroke.

Setup: A full-length mirror and a baseball bat.

Procedure: Assume batting stance as if the mirror were the pitcher. Go through your swing in slow motion. Say aloud the different hitting stages — stance, stride, pivot, swing, follow-through.Verbalizing reinforces the natural sequence and promotes good muscle memory. Watch yourself in the mirror for the entire swing process. After a few swings, pick up the pace. After fifteen to twenty swings, the player should be at full speed.

Coach's Note: The mirror is an effective teaching tool and can be used in many of the other drills. The mirror helps the player to see mistakes that the coach has pointed out. By observing what the coach has noticed, the player can develop a "feel." The notion of getting a "feel" and connecting the visual process with the coach's comments and corrective strategies is essential for correcting errors.

#2 — HIP TURN DRILL

Objective: To practice the back side pivot.
To generate explosive hip action.

Setup: You need only a bat, although this drill is best done in front of a mirror.

Procedure: Place the bat behind your back horizontally, and just above the waist. Hold the bat with the insides of your elbows by pulling it into your back. Take your stride and then turn your hips to initiate the pivot. The pivot action should start at a controlled pace to confirm the correct mechanics of the movement. As you become familiar with the action and the drill, speed up so that the explosive and quick turning of the hips emerges.

Coach's Note: Reinforce the concept of "squishing the fly." Upon completion of a repetition, check to see if the hitter's belly button is facing the pitcher. The front leg should be firm and locked. The "L" shape of the back leg must be noticeable. The player should be trying to generate bat speed with his hips.

Hip Turn Drill

Variation: Hold the bat in the same way but at such a height that the barrel will move over the plate when the pivot is completed. Place a ball on a tee no more than one foot away from your body. The tee should also be at the height of your bat. Complete the hip turn and attempt to knock the ball off the tee.

#3 — BALANCE DRILL

Objective: To develop balance in the batting swing.

Setup: This drill should initially be performed with a tee. Progress to soft toss as balance improves. Stand with each foot on a block the size of a cement cinder block used in most commercial construction. Each block is about one foot long, 8 inches wide, and 8 inches high. Position the blocks perpendicular to each other. The block underneath your back foot will

Balance Drill

be set up similar to the shape of your foot. Turn the front block in the opposite direction to allow for the forward movement of the stride foot.

Procedure: Take your stride to assume the load position. Swing and hit the ball off the tee or the feed from your partner. Upon making contact, finish your swing and follow through. Complete the entire swing process and remain on the blocks.

Coach's Note: The balance blocks are excellent means to illustrate the importance of balance to the hitter. They can also serve as a self-corrective measure because the hitter will adjust in an effort to achieve the balance needed to stay on the blocks. Eventually you want the drill performed at game-like speed.

#4 – PIVOT BOARD DRILL

Objective: To develop complete back side pivoting action.

Setup: A pivot board is needed for this drill. A pivot board consists of a thick piece of plywood (approximately 3 feet wide and 5 feet long) fastened to a border or frame of two-by-fours. At one end of the plywood, a hole is cut out and the cut out piece is then fastened to a "lazy susan" device. The lazy susan is a bracket (sold at most hardware stores) which permits a complete 360 degree turn. The circle should turn freely. These pivot boards are available at several sporting goods stores or through some mail-order companies.

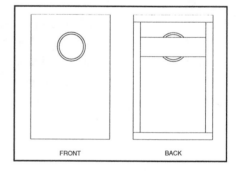

FRONT   BACK

The pivot board

You can build your own pivot board at a much cheaper cost, and with limited skills and effort.

Procedure: Start with your back foot on the circle part of the pivot board. The ball of your foot will be placed directly on the centre of the rotating part of the board. Take your stride and then hit the ball off the tee or the toss from your partner. Your back foot should turn freely to enable a complete back side pivot.

Coach's Note: Make sure the hitter's belly button finishes by facing the field. The pivot board should make it easy for the hitter to develop explosive hip action and bat speed. Look for the "squishing of the fly," and the "heel to the sky."

#5 — PIVOT TURN DRILL

Objective: To demonstrate the full backside pivot.

Setup: Drill requires a tee and some baseballs.

Procedure: Place tee a few feet from the fence. Start with your back to the fence. Your front foot should be 8 to 12 inches from the base of the tee and your weight should be primarily on the back leg. Your partner will yell "pivot," and you will turn and drive the ball into the screen.

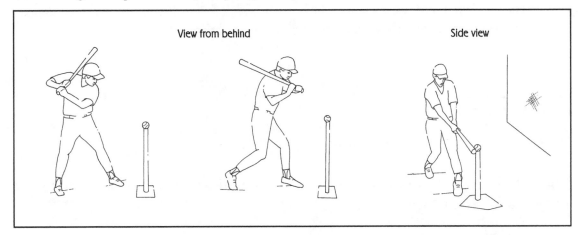

View from behind   Side view

Pivot Turn Drill

Coach's Note: This drill is very effective for getting players to complete the pivoting action. Check to see that the front leg locks out and keeps the weight back. Tee location is crucial to this drill. Do not place the tee too far in front or else the hitter will bend her front leg and lunge to reach the baseball. If the tee is too close to the front leg, the hitter may have to collapse her back side in order to maintain enough distance to make solid contact. Experiment with the tee location until you find the ideal spot.

Variation: The Pivot Turn Drill can also be performed in a soft toss format.

#6 — VISION DRILL I

Objective: To develop the ability to recognize different pitch locations.

Setup: Pitcher will throw to catcher. Hitter will stand in the batter's box.

Procedure: Watch the ball leave the pitcher's hand. Determine the type of pitch, as well as the location, as quickly as possible. Use one-syllable verbal cues to save time. As the ball approaches, call out the pitch and location. For example, you might say "fast, strike," to indicate that the pitch selection was a fastball and the location was not in the strike zone. Similarly, "curve, ball," suggests that the pitch was a curve ball out of the zone. Shout these verbal cues as soon as possible.

Coach's Note: Many hitters have no idea about the details of the pitch even if they hit it. Pitch recognition is extremely helpful to those players who have the tendency to chase balls that are out of the strike zone. It doesn't matter which word is stated first. If you feel that location is a greater concern for your team, have your players yell out location first.

#7 — VISION DRILL II

Objective: To improve pitch recognition abilities.

Setup: Number six to nine baseballs with a marker. This drill can be conducted in soft toss or live batting practice environments.

Procedure: The hitter will use solid hitting mechanics to make contact with each feed. After making contact, the hitter will call out the number he saw on the baseball. (Number the ball several times to increase visibility.)

Coach's Note: Since the rotation will not be as tight on soft-toss feeds, coaches are encouraged to use soft toss when first introducing this drill. As players become more adept at seeing the rotation, progress to a batting practice situation. If the batting-practice pitcher throws with a tight rotation on her ball, players may not be able to identify the numbers. Even so, since they'll be concentrating on the pitch in an effort to determine the number, the objective of the drill — pitch recognition — will be met.

#8 – POINTS OF CONTACT DRILL

Objective: To understand the different points of contact for different pitch locations.

Setup: A batting tee, baseball, and home plate are needed for this drill.

Procedure: Place the tee 8 to 12 inches in front of home plate in line with the inside corner. You will swing and pull the ball to simulate an inside pitch. Move the tee back so that it's two to four inches in front of home plate, but in line with the middle. You will swing and hit the ball up the middle to simulate pitches thrown down the heart of the plate. Then move the tee to the outside part of the plate where it begins to angle to a point. In this setup, you will make contact deeper in your body and hit the outside pitch the other way. Each player should take two swings at each location before switching.

Coach's Note: Regardless of the pitch location, the hitter's swing shouldn't alter. Only the point of contact should vary with the different positions of the tee.

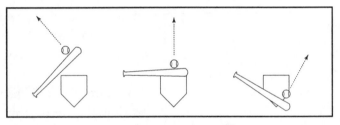

Points of Contact Drill

#9 – TWO TEE LOCATION DRILL

Objective: To hit the ball where it is pitched.
To develop bat control over the various parts of the strike zone.

Setup: Two tees are needed for this drill. Position the first about 8 to 12 inches in front of the plate, in line with the inside corner. Set the second on the back outside corner of the plate. The inside tee should be set up lower than the outside tee by about 6 inches. The height difference must be enough to accommodate the width of your bat. When swinging at the outside pitch your bat must be able to pass above the ball on top of the inside tee.

Procedure: Begin your stance. Your partner will tell you to "stride." If your stride is performed correctly, your partner will follow this command by instructing you to hit one of the balls. He will state either "inside" or "outside." You will follow this command and pivot to hit the appropriate ball.

Two Tee Location Drill

Coach's Note: The mechanics of the swing should not change based on the pitch location. If the swing is level, the other tee should not be affected by a swing, so only one ball should be hit off the tee per swing.

#10 — TWO TEE TARGET DRILL

Objective: To hit the ball hard up the middle.
          To hit line drives.

Setup: Two batting tees are required. Place the first tee slightly in front of home plate by 2 to 4 inches. Line it up with the middle of the plate. The second tee should be placed at least two feet in front of the first tee in a direct line at the same height. Place a ball on both tees.

Procedure: You will assume a ready position. Your partner will provide the verbal hitting commands — stride and pivot. Attempt to hit the ball off the first tee so that it makes contact with the ball on the second tee. The ball on the front tee serves as a target.

Coach's Note: As your hitters become more successful, move the front tee further ahead. You may want to set up competitions to determine who can hit the most targets. For advanced hitters, leave the front tee in the original position and have the partner feed soft toss. The hitter will try to hit the feed and knock the ball off the front tee.

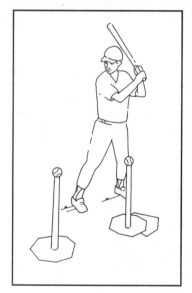

Two Tee Target Drill

#11 — SHORT TOSS DRILL

Objective: To become comfortable hitting the ball as pitched.
          To separate the stride and swing.
          To develop plate awareness.

Setup: The "L" screen (fencing which protects the pitcher) should be placed about 10 feet away from home plate. Be sure there are no holes in the screen. The tosser will sit on a chair or bucket behind the screen with several baseballs available.

Procedure: The tosser will make an underhand flip so that only her arm is outside the screen. The toss should be firm, on a straight line, and without a loop. After releasing the ball, the tosser must bring her arm behind the screen to avoid injury. You will take your stride as the arm of the tosser moves. With your stride already completed, you're in the load position and ready to attack the ball if it's a strike. Feeds should be directed to the various parts of the strike zone. Only swing at strikes.

Short Toss Drill

Coach's Note: Short toss is a necessary component of any team or program. With this drill, there is no need to worry about a batting practice pitcher. Every player on your team should be able to throw underhand strikes from ten feet away. Short toss is one of the best methods of maximizing swings in a short period of time. This way you're not wasting time waiting for the pitcher to throw strikes. Pitchers won't tire since they can throw this way all day long. The velocity of the feeds must coincide with the type of pitching your team will face in a game. The hitter should use the moving arm of the feeder to develop her timing, as she would to the arm action of the pitcher when she is on the mound. Furthermore, the underhand feed forces you to stay on top of the ball for solid contact.

Variation: Short toss is used in conjunction with other drills featured in this chapter. Due to the relative simplicity of this drill, it can also be used to work on different types of pitches. (see Off-speed Drill, Wait Drill).

#12 — EYES CLOSED DRILL

Objective: To visualize the ball.
     To make the swing automatic, developing solid muscle memory.

Setup: A tee and a few baseballs are all that is needed for this drill.

Procedure: Place a ball on the tee and prepare to hit. Once you feel ready and have had a long look at the baseball, close your eyes. Picture the ball in your mind. With eyes closed, stride and swing to strike the baseball.

Coach's Note: The Eyes Closed Drill is demanding, so it will be popular with players while refining their hitting mechanics.

#13 – SHOULDER TO SHOULDER DRILL

Objective: To swing the bat the entire route.
To eliminate a loop in the swing.

Setup: This drill can be set up using a tee or soft toss.

Procedure: Use a touch system as a starting point. Rest your bat against the corner of your back shoulder. The corner of your shoulder refers to the furthest point moving across the shoulder before your arm starts to go down. Keep the bat at this point, even during the stride. When you begin the swing take your bat from the back shoulder through the ball to your front shoulder. Feel the bat make contact at three points – back shoulder, baseball, and front shoulder.

Coach's Note: During the drill, ask the hitter if he felt all three contact points. This self-check will assist him in focusing on the bat going the entire route. Throughout the swing, the bat speed should not decrease. In other words, the bat must not only travel the complete distance, it must also be quick the entire way. Young or inexperienced players may have a habit of slowing up their bat upon contact.

#14 – LEVEL SWING DRILL

Objective: To keep the bat level during your swing.
To develop a line drive swing.

Setup: Place two tees in line with each other in the middle of the plate. Place a ball on top of the two tees at the same height. The tees should be relatively close together (approximately 8 inches apart).

Procedure: Swing and attempt to knock both balls off with the same stroke. If the bat loops, only one ball will be hit and you'll know the bat was not level during the swing.

Coach's Note: You can widen the space between the tees, but not so much that the player must lunge for the ball. In the Two Tee Target Drill, the hitter is trying to hit the first ball so that it will knock the other ball off the tee.

#15 — SHADOW DRILL

Objective: To keep the head still and prevent too much forward movement.

Setup: Stand with your back to the sun so that your shadow falls in front of you.

Procedure: Watch the head of your shadow. Take a stride and then swing, saying the hitting terms to yourself while performing the drill. Throughout this swing, watch for any forward movement of your head. If you have trouble watching for this movement, place a baseball or glove on the ground at the spot where your shadow's head rests. At the conclusion of your swing, it will be easier to determine if the head stayed still. Since your weight shift is back and then to the middle, your head should not move forward past your body centre.

Coach's Note: Don't mistake head rotation for linear movement. The head's rotation during the swing is natural. When teaching the importance of preventing linear movement prior to contact, remind your hitters that the head moves forward at approximately 3 to 5 miles an hour, which computes directly into additional velocity for the incoming pitch.

Variation: If the day is cloudy, this drill can be done in front of a mirror. Place a piece of tape in the middle of the mirror at the same height as your cap. Line up the middle of your cap with this piece of tape to determine if undesirable movement took place.

#16 — TOSS FROM BEHIND DRILL

Objective: To increase bat speed and explosive hip action.
To eliminate the "loop" from a swing.

Setup: Set up facing the screen, or netting, with your partner behind home plate. The feeder, your partner, will be kneeling about six feet behind the plate with some balls.

Toss from Behind Drill

Procedure: Turn your head slightly, just enough to see the feeder out of the corner of your eye. Your partner will instruct you to stride and then toss the ball. Once the ball enters the hitting zone, attempt to hit it. Take the bat straight to the ball. A poor path will not allow the bat to catch up.

Coach's Note: If the batter has a loop in her swing, she will never catch up to the ball. This drill forces hitters to take the bat straight to the ball in order to make contact. Advanced hitters should request the feed to be harder with less loft to further improve bat speed. Don't allow the hitter to turn her head all the way around to watch the feed.

Variation: Younger players may have to place the feeder behind at a 45-degree angle before moving her straight behind. The angle makes contact easier.

#17 – OVERHEAD DROP DRILL

Objective: To improve bat speed.

Setup: Place a chair or short ladder in the batter's box opposite the hitter.

Overhead Drop Drill

Procedure: Your partner will stand on the chair and instruct you to stride. Upon completing your stride, your partner will drop a ball into the hitting zone from above. You must explode your hips to generate the bat speed necessary to make contact.

Coach's Note: Due to the difficulty of this drill, I wouldn't recommend it for young hitters, who may become quickly discouraged. Wait until they become more adept hitters and are in need of additional challenges.

#18 — WAIT DRILL

Objective: To learn to wait until the ball enters your strong zone.
To effectively hit the ball to the opposite field.

Setup: This drill is performed in a short toss situation. Don't pitch from the full distance, so that the pitcher can more consistently locate the ball on the outside corner. Move the "L" screen up to at least half distance or more. The drill can also be performed in batting practice.

Procedure: The pitcher will place every toss on the outer half of the plate. You will watch the first few pitches without swinging but yell "swing" at the exact moment when you must start your swing. Hit outside pitches to the opposite field. Going the other way with the pitch is achieved by making contact deeper in the hitting zone without modifying the swing. So if you want to make contact deeper in the zone, you must still begin your swing early enough to get the barrel of the bat on the ball. After watching a few tosses, you can start swinging to hit every pitch to the opposite field. Use a six-pitch round consisting of three observations and three swings.

Coach's Note: The players should discover just how long they can wait before swinging. Don't permit players to alter their swing to hit the ball the other way. The strong zone of hitting happens when the top arm is bent at contact.

#19 — TIRE DRILL

Objective: To develop strong arms, wrists and forearms.
To swing the bat the entire route.

Setup: Puncture a rubber tire. Slide the tire over top of a pole, as pictured in the diagram. Pin or clamp the tire at the desired height so that it spins freely around the pole. You may want to use one of your older bats for this exercise.

Procedure: Focus on the tire, swing your bat, making sure to follow through. Try to increase the number of times the tire can completely spin around.

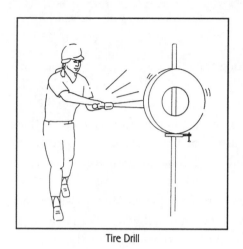

Tire Drill

Coach's Note: Make sure you can adjust height of the tire.

#20 – RESISTANCE DRILL

Objective: To build strength in arms, wrists, and forearms.

Setup: You'll need a partner and one bat.

Procedure: Take your stance. Your partner will stand to the side with his hands on the end of the bat. As you swing, your partner will resist by pushing against the bat.

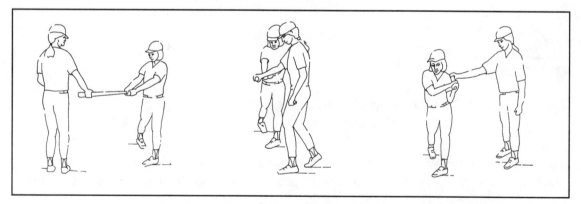

Resistance Drill

Coach's Note: The partner can also help the hitter to take a straight route to the ball. Don't let the batter loop his swing.

#21 — TOP HAND HITTING DRILL

Objective: To teach the importance of bent arms at contact.
To illustrate the effectiveness of hitting down on the baseball.

Setup: To prevent injury, use a bat about 6 inches shorter than what you would use in a game.

Procedure: Use your top hand to hit the baseball. If right-handed, use your right hand, if left-handed, hit with only your left hand on the bat. Your other hand will be near the bat but not holding it. Otherwise, hit as usual, without modifying your swing. Try to stay on top of the ball and hit line drives and ground balls.

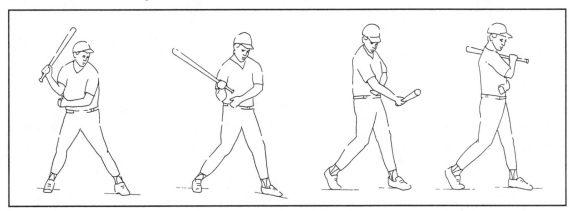

Top Hand Hitting Drill

Coach's Note: If the hitter tries to lift the ball by dropping the bat head, or if the bat moves away from her body, she may see a noticeable drop in power. Hard-hit balls should result from swinging down on the ball. Make sure the player keeps the arm bent and the bat reasonably close to the body when making contact. Make sure they do not roll the wrist prior to contact.

#22 — BOTTOM HAND HITTING DRILL

Objective: To establish that the bottom hand is responsible for the direction of the bat to the ball.

Setup: Again, use a bat 6 inches shorter than your regular one. Your partner will feed soft toss or short toss.

Procedure: This drill is the same as the Top Hand Hitting Drill, except that you hold the bat with your bottom hand. If right-handed, keep your left hand on the bat, while lefties will use their right hand. Using regular swing mechanics, try to stay on top and hit down on the baseball.

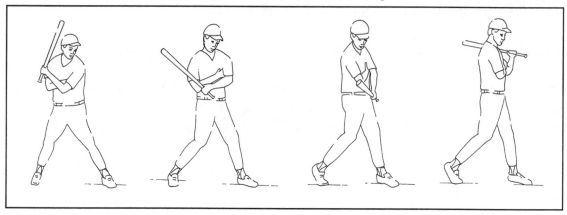

Bottom Hand Hitting Drill

Coach's Note: The bottom hand is responsible for the direction of the swing. For this reason, don't be concerned with how hard the ball is hit. The goal is to establish solid contact due to a firm directional hand. Discourage modification of the player's swing.

#23 — CHAIR DRILL

Objective: To teach the concept of "chopping the tree."
To produce ground balls and line drives.

Setup: The tee location isn't important for the Chair Drill, as long as it falls within the distance established by the player's feet. Avoid placing it in front of the lead foot. Set up an aluminum, plastic, or wooden folding chair about one foot behind the tee. Lower the tee so the ball is an inch or two below the chair height. Again, using an old bat might be best.

Procedure: Swing and strike the ball without hitting the chair. Swing on a downward angle. Any lift in the swing or uppercut action will result in contact with the chair before the bat can even reach the ball. The obstacle of the chair produces a direct path for the bat.

Coach's Note: To prove the effectiveness of this drill, have the players check the point where the ball hits the screen. In each situation, it will be a line drive or ground ball.

Variation: You can use a tee in place of the chair. While your bat's contact with the chair will notify everyone in the area that you took a less than direct route to the ball, the tee will cause less damage to the bat. In either situation, the hitting objectives are accomplished.

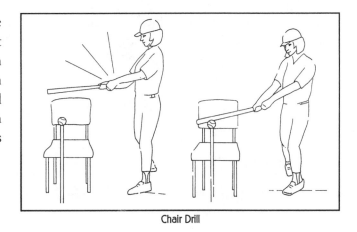

Chair Drill

#24 — ONE KNEE CHOP DRILL

Objective: To achieve the downward angle of the swing.

Setup: Start with your back knee on the ground and your front leg straight out to the side. Don't rest on your back ankle. Remain as upright and erect as possible. Assume the upper body portion of your stance. Hands will be at your back shoulder, at shoulder height. Your bat's knob will point at the opposite batter's box. Your partner should place the tee directly underneath and just below your hands.

Procedure: Your partner will feed you with a soft toss, each toss below the height of the tee. Lobbing the ball above the tee and letting it drop will defeat the purpose of the drill. Feeds should also be directed just above the front knee, which is positioned straight out to the side. Use only your upper body to swing and take your bat straight to the ball. Concentrate on finishing your swing by taking the bat all the way to your back shoulder. If you loop

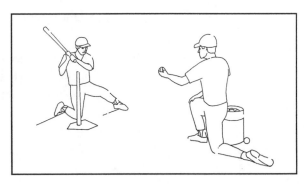

One Knee Chop Drill

your bat or drop your hands, the bat will strike the tee and prevent contact with the ball.

Coach's Note: The One Knee Chop Drill is extremely effective for establishing the correct path for the bat. The hitter gets immediate feedback regarding the route of her bat since, if her bat loops, solid contact is impossible. The feeder plays an important role in this drill. If he doesn't make quality feeds, the drill falls flat. Also, if the hitter doesn't follow through, her bat will fall after contact and hit her front leg. Make hitters concentrate on finishing the swing at the back and side of their front shoulders.

#25 — PUSH/PULL DRILL

Objective: To define the roles of the two hands during the swing.
To eliminate a loop in the player's swing.

Setup: Start the Push/Pull Drill by using a tee and then progress to a soft toss format. Your grip on the bat is very unorthodox for this drill. Take your top hand and turn it over so that your thumb points down. Your bat should rest against the palm of the top hand, which will be four to 6 inches higher up on the bat. Sliding your top hand up the handle will allow for additional bat control. Your top hand won't grip the bat. Don't wrap your fingers around the handle. Rather, let the bat rest against your palm. With your top hand positioned in such a manner, your back elbow will automatically be high.

Push/Pull Drill

Procedure: Though your grip is irregular, hit as usual. If using the tee, vocalize the commands to yourself to ensure separation of the stride and swing. During soft toss, have your partner give the commands. As you swing, your bottom hand is responsible for direction, pulling the bat straight to the ball. Your top hand asserts power by pushing the bat through the ball. It should push the bat with such force that you finish with only one hand on the bat. If you attempt a two-handed finish using this grip, the swing will be shortened, so release the bat from the top hand.

Coach's Note: This drill will clearly define the different roles of the player's hands. Monitor the unusual grip and prevent hitters from wrapping the fingers of the top hand around the handle. Power can be achieved from this type of swing only if the bat is directed through the correct route to the ball. If the hitter tries to lift the ball or uppercut, contact is weak. The top hand should make a powerful thrust on the bat. Generate explosive pushing force from this part of the swing.

#26 — BALL THROWING DRILL

Objective: To get the barrel of the bat on the ball by getting the bat head into the hitting zone. To illustrate the point of extension after contact.

Setup: Have a baseball in each hand and assume batting stance, facing a screen or netting. Position the baseballs to resemble the bat, with one hand with a ball on top of the other.

Procedure: Take your normal swing. As your hands approach an imaginary point of contact, release the baseballs and extend your arms to follow-through. If good bat speed has been achieved, the baseballs should hit the fence with significant force. The arms will behave much as with a throwing action. If the balls don't hit the fence in front of the hitter, then the barrel of the bat did not effectively get out front when you hit the ball.

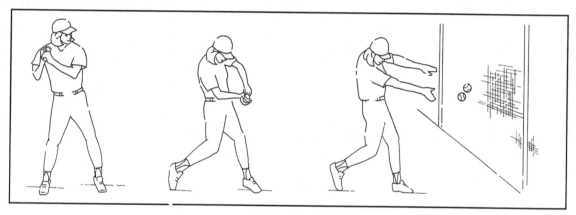

Ball Throwing Drill

Coach's Note: Challenge the hitters to get power out of the Throwing Drill. This power can only be achieved if the balls are released with the top hand still bent. If the player waits until his arms are at maximum extension and completely straight, he is beginning to lose some power. The arms will get to this extension point, but not prior to contact. Also, make sure the hitters are throwing the balls to simulate a line drive or ground ball. Trying for home run swings during drill work will only promote bad habits.

#27 – THROW THE BAT HEAD DRILL

Objective: To achieve extension of the arms after contact.
To get the barrel of the bat slightly out front at contact.

Setup: Using an old bat, stand at an angle to the screen or net. The angle must be such that your body and the screen would eventually merge into a point.

Procedure: Take a regular cut at an imaginary pitch. At the point of contact, throw your bat into the screen or net. Your arms will continue through to the finishing point. The bat should hit the fence with considerable impact and noise. Try for as much noise as possible and think of it as power in your swing.

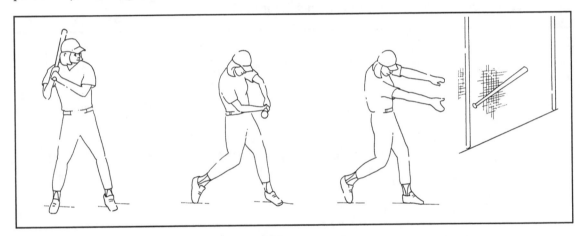

Throw the Bat Head Drill

Coach's Note: This drill will help players recognize maximum power. If the bat head gets too far out in front, power is diminished because the arms are no longer in a position of strength. If the bat head falls short, bat speed is slowed. The point at which arms reach extension should be a 45-degree angle. Thus, the ultimate power zone is prior to that 45-degree angle and before the arms are fully extended. Encourage hitters to use this drill to develop the "feel" for their power zones.

#28 — INWARD TURN DRILL

Objective: To keep the front shoulder closed.
To prevent the hitter from pulling her front side.
To stay through the ball during the swing.

Setup: Stand with toes pointing into the screen or net. Your body should be positioned in a line parallel to the screen. The tee will be placed or the partner will kneel beside your back foot.

Procedure: Take your stance and then start the drill by taking an exaggerated inward turn so your shoulders are now pointing into the screen. The inward turn will allow you to see the feeder or tee. As you turn, your partner will flip a toss. Pivot on your back foot and drive the ball into the screen.

Inward Turn Drill

Coach's Note: The stride is eliminated from this drill. The feeder/partner should try to establish a rhythm so that it won't be necessary for the hitter to hold turned shoulders. The movement should be smooth, shoulders rotating to swing and then following through back to the starting point. The smoothness of the inward turn assists the hitter with timing and is most helpful when the feeder establishes a rhythm.

#29 — RAPID FIRE DRILL

Objective: To improve bat speed.
To rehearse the most direct route to the ball.

Setup: Get to your stride point and assume the load position. Your partner should have several balls ready in front of him. The stride is eliminated from this drill.

Procedure: Your partner will flip the ball in a basic soft toss. You must pivot to hit the baseball. As soon as you've reached the finishing point — the front shoulder — your partner flips another ball. You must take a direct route to the ball and the same direct route back to load position.

Your partner will feed five consecutive tosses in this fashion before switching up. If your bat takes a bad path to the ball, you'll notice difficulty catching up with the next pitch. Your objective is to take a consistent and straight route to the ball. This drill resembles the Shoulder to Shoulder Drill but is in continuous motion, and without the stride. The flow of movement should follow a pattern of pivot - swing - finish - reload - pivot - swing - finish - reload.

Coach's Note: Don't exceed five feeds during the Rapid Fire Drill. Hitters will tire easily with only five tosses, so any more risks the development of ineffective habits. Ideally, as the hitter gets quicker and increases her bat speed, the feeder will speed up. The two should develop timing and rhythm to maximize the effectiveness of the drill.

Variation: Rapid Fire can also be applied to work solely on the route of your bat by placing you on one knee. This modified version of the drill focuses strictly on your upper body and eliminates the pivoting action. This is a good drill for younger players, because there are fewer moves to concentrate on. (See #24 — One Knee Chop Drill.)

#30 — COLOUR DRILL

Objective: To keep your eyes focused on the ball.
   To improve vision and concentration during the hitting process.

Setup: The feeder will kneel down across from you with a bucket of balls of different colours. You can use tennis balls, rubber balls, whiffle balls, or ball hockey balls for this drill.

Procedure: The feeder will place two different coloured balls into the palm of his hand so that you can see them, then he will instruct you to stride. Upon completion of a correct stride, the feeder will call out one of the colours and then flip both balls into the hitting zone. You will pivot and hit the ball as called. The feeder must call the colour early enough to give you a chance to swing. For example, the feeder might have a white baseball and a yellow tennis ball in his hand. He will grip them side by side with the palm up. As both balls are flipped into the air, he yells "yellow," which cues you to hit the yellow tennis ball.

Coach's Note: Use this drill often in practice; players love it. The colour drill offers an alternative to standard soft toss, and is excellent for improving visual skills.

#31 – TOP / BOTTOM DRILL

Objective: To keep your eyes on the ball.
To improve vision and concentration during the hitting process.

Setup: The feeder will kneel down with a bucket of balls in similar fashion to the Colour Drill. The balls don't have to be different colours.

Procedure: Your partner will place two balls into the palm of her hand so that you can see them. Her hand should hold the balls with the thumb pointing up so that the balls sit on top of one another. She will instruct you to stride. Upon completion of a correct stride, your partner calls out one of the balls by its location and then flips both balls into the hitting zone. You will pivot and hit the ball as called. Again, your partner will call the ball early enough to give you a chance to swing. For example, as both balls are flipped into the air, your partner yells "top," which tells you to hit the ball that was on top when your partner held them in her hand. If your partner does her job correctly, the balls should travel in the same relationship that they started. In other words, the ball placed on top in your partner's hand should travel through the air higher than the bottom ball. This relationship is achieved by your partner making smooth flips with her arm. She must keep her hand still in order to avoid altering the path of either ball.

Coach's Note: The Colour Drill involved selecting and hitting balls that were on different horizontal paths. The Top/Bottom Drill deals with differences in pitch heights or vertical paths. The player will be hitting a ball higher or lower, as opposed to inside or out. This drill simply changes the focus point for the hitter.

#32 – GOOD BALL / BAD BALL DRILL

Objective: To be selective at the plate and avoid chasing pitches that are out of the strike zone.

Setup: A partner will kneel down beside home plate in standard soft toss format. He will need lots of balls.

Procedure: Your feeder/partner holds a ball in each hand and moves them in a circular fashion away and then back to his body. The circle action should not be in unison. As one ball is at the

Good Ball/Bad Ball Drill

top of the circle, the other one should be at the bottom. You will have already taken your stride. Throughout the entire drill, remain in the load position until you swing. Foot movement is eliminated with the exception of the back side pivot. Your eyes must focus on the two balls in constant motion. The feeder will, after a few circles, toss the balls, half of them in and half out of the strike zone. The feeder will not stop the hand circles even when he makes a toss. The hand which still holds a ball will continue circling while the other hand reaches down to pick up a new ball and re-enters the circle. His hands will keep circling and flipping the ball intermittently. Be selective. Swing at pitches in the zone, and let bad pitches go by.

Coach's Note: The Good Ball/Bad Ball Drill is an outstanding method for teaching discipline at the plate. In a very compact setting, the hitter is forced to be aggressive on strikes while leaving bad pitches alone. Most hitting drills feature good pitches and put the hitter in a habit of swinging at everything. While this feature helps to teach players to be aggressive at the plate, the Good Ball/Bad Ball Drill effectively includes discipline and awareness of the strike zone. Instruct the feeder to avoid being predictable. The hitter shouldn't know what to expect.

#33 — BREAKING BALL DRILL

Objective: To teach hitters to stay back on the curve ball.
To hit breaking pitches the opposite way.

Setup: Your partner kneels down at a 45-degree angle from your front foot. If you are right-handed, imagine you are standing in the middle of a clock, your partner will be located between 10 and 11 o'clock. He is on your back side, without being directly behind you.

Procedure: Take your stride according to your partner's verbal instructions. When you complete a proper stride, your partner will toss a ball across your front leg into the hitting zone. The feeds should be lofted to simulate the dropping of the curve ball. Keep your weight back and then explode your hips to attack the ball. Try to hit the off-speed pitch hard to the opposite field.

Coach's Note: The best approach to hitting off-speed pitches is to wait longer and then explode the hips. The swing should not be modified for off-speed pitches. The reason for separating the stride and swing is to give the hitter the opportunity to hit the off-speed pitch. As long as he keeps his weight and hands back, he can still hit the ball hard. It isn't essential that all breaking pitches be hit to the opposite field. Encourage going the other way in this drill so that players learn to wait. The biggest problem in facing off-speed pitches is the tendency for players to lunge for the ball. If you tell your hitter to go the opposite way and he

Breaking Ball Drill

still commits early, there is a chance that he could pull the ball fair. If, however, his objective is to pull a curve ball, committing early will permit only a foul ball, if any contact at all.

#34 — SHORT TOSS OFF-SPEED DRILL

Objective: To keep the hands and weight back on off-speed pitches.
To hit off-speed pitches hard.

Setup: Using the short toss setup, your partner kneels behind a protective screen about ten feet away from you. Make sure there are no holes in the screen (as with #11 — Short Toss Drill).

Procedure: Using an underhand flip toss, your partner tosses the ball into the hitting zone. These feeds must be firm and on a line to the plate. Every few pitches, your partner lofts a feed into the air to simulate an off-speed pitch. She can masquerade her intentions by changing the release point and maintaining arm speed. When participating in short toss drills, use your partner's arm as a timing mechanism for the stride. As her arm moves forward, make your stride. If the feed is a straight "fastball," you'll be in the load position and ready to explode the hips. If the feed is an "off-speed pitch," wait a little longer in the load position before swinging.

Coach's Note: Finding a batting-practice pitcher who can throw breaking balls consistently for strikes is not easy. Every player on your team can vary the speed in a short toss. Some variation in the pitches is all that's needed to teach hitters to keep their hands and weight back.

#35 — FENCE DRILL

Objective: To reinforce a short compact swing.

To prevent hitters from lunging at the pitch.

To prevent your hands from getting away from your body.

Setup: Facing a fence or screen, hold your bat horizontally from your belly button to the fence. The bat length establishes your distance from the screen. Your body should be positioned so that your shoulders run parallel with the screen while toes are pointing towards it. An older bat is recommended for initial experiences with this drill.

Procedure: Focus your eyes on an imaginary pitcher. Swing the bat hard without making contact with the fence. If your arms get too far away from your body, the bat will bang into the screen. Keep your swing short and compact with arms comfortably bent at the elbow to swing through.

Fence Drill

Coach's Note: Hitters should not be permitted to modify their swing in order to avoid contact with the fence. Instructing players to keep the arms bent doesn't imply they should be in tight to the body. Make sure they reach extension after contact. Dry swings during the Fence Drill can produce some very short and compact strokes capable of tremendous power.

#36 – NO STRIDE DRILL

Objective: To develop a feel for the proper weight transfer back to the load position.
To practice staying closed.
To isolate upper body movements.

Setup: Use a tee or soft toss with the No Stride Drill. If using a tee, place it between the feet and vary height and location. If the drill features a soft toss partner, then he should be kneeling in the opposite batter's box.

Procedure: Shift your weight back to the load position and then pivot to hit the ball. Your weight transfer should also include getting your hands started. Your lower body doesn't move through the drill, with the exception of the pivot. Even then, your feet don't leave the ground. Focus on the fundamentals of the swing. On completion of your swing, your weight should shift back to the middle.

Coach's Note: The No Stride Drill is *not* a hitting approach. It should be used only for the purpose stated above. As a drill, the no stride method is an effective learning tool. As an approach to hitting, it lacks power, timing, and bat speed. No stride hitting makes it easy for the player to hit the ball, but the hitter's goal should be to hit the ball hard, not just connect.

Variation: The No Stride Drill can be used in many of the previous drills. Use the drill to isolate certain movements, or to concentrate on other aspects of the swing, by not focusing on lower-body actions.

SIXTH INNING
BUNTING

BUNTING

Bunting has become a lost art in the game of baseball.
                      — Rod Carew, *The Art and Science of Hitting*

Bunting is one of baseball's most basic skills and yet seems to have become something of a lost art. Players are no longer necessarily capable of executing a bunt when it's most needed. The 1996 World Series is an excellent example. Mark Lemke of the Atlanta Braves was heralded as a clutch offensive performer. Yet he was unable to successfully execute a bunt and move the runner on first to second base. While there were many reasons for the Braves' failure to win the Series, many analysts suggest that this bad bunt was the turning point in the fall classic.

The glory of hitting the long ball has eclipsed the importance of the bunt. Often, players either refuse or make a half-hearted attempt when called upon to bunt. In some instances, it may be understandable. If fans pay forty-five dollars a game to watch Ken Griffey Jr. play, they don't want to see him lay down a sacrifice bunt. Major League baseball is an entertainment industry, but most often, fans are parents and friends who want to see the whole team win. And, bunting can be a major component of winning ball games.

Although bunting may not be the biggest part of offence, it is a necessary ingredient, so use it often in practice. Give players the opportunity to swing the bat too, since that's why most kids play the game. As players age and gain a better understanding at the plate, the importance of the bunt is even greater and, as Lemke can attest, can be the difference between winning and losing the game.

Reward quality bunts in practice by giving the player extra swings. If the player bunts well, give him extra time in the batting tunnel. If he doesn't progress, reduce or eliminate his swings. Try to place the hitter in a stressful bunting situation, and observe his performance. Be consistent with this system, even with your number four hitter who might not bunt the entire season. You never know when he may be called on to execute a perfect bunt.

The most effective bunt is down the third base line. The long throw by the third baseman allows for a greater possibility of error, especially if he is hurried. This means you have more time to reach first base. A bunt down the first base line requires a shorter throw, maybe an off-balance toss or the glove shovelling the ball, making it easier to record the out.

This doesn't mean you should completely avoid bunting down the first baseline; some left-handed hitters have made a living dragging the ball down the line to first. But since there are more right-handed pitchers, who tend to fall towards the first base side of the infield, it's easier to keep the ball away from them when you bunt to third. At the younger levels, keeping the ball away from the pitcher is a great advantage because youth pitchers are often the top athletes on the team and it's best to keep the ball out of their hands.

In this chapter, I'll discuss the sacrifice bunt, bunting for a hit by a right-handed hitter, and bunting for a hit by a left-handed hitter. I'll also discuss the two prevalent theories regarding the sacrifice bunt. Finally, you'll find several drills that are instructive and fun.

SQUARING TO BUNT vs. THE PIVOT METHOD

The sacrifice bunt is an offensive tool intended to move the base runner one base. For example, if the team needs a run to tie the game, with no outs and a runner on first, they might consider a sacrifice bunt to move the runner to second where she can score on a single. This is referred to as a "sacrifice" because the hitter will exchange her out to move the runner to second.

There are two common approaches to the sacrifice bunt — squaring to bunt, and the pivot method. Squaring to bunt implies that the hitter turnd her body so she is squared, toes pointed at the pitcher. The pivot method involves keeping your feet still but shifting your body by pivoting on the balls of your feet so that your upper body is opened up to the pitcher.

There are some drawbacks in squaring to bunt. As you can see from the diagram, you are fully exposed, and extremely vulnerable to a ball thrown directly at you. Because you've turned and squared your feet, they are planted. Which way can you move? Not only are you stuck, but your face, rib cage, neck, and groin are exposed to the oncoming ball. If a young player gets hit in the face or chest from a pitched ball, he may develop a fear of hitting. There's nothing worse (not even a rain-out!) for a baseball player than fear of the ball.

The pivot method, on the other hand, places you in a more athletic position, and you can escape more easily from a ball thrown at you. Because you pivoted to get to the bunting position you can pivot back to avoid the baseball. By pivoting back, chances are the ball will impact on the back side of your body where the muscles groups are larger, and your vital organs and joints are protected.

You will be hit by a pitch at some point in your baseball career. The coach's job is to help you get into a position where you can avoid getting hit, or conquer any injuries or mental blocks that result from getting hit. A large bruise on the butt is easier to rebound from than a broken wrist.

Squaring to Bunt   The Pivot Method

THE SACRIFICE BUNT

When sacrifice bunting, you're not trying to fool the defense, so it doesn't matter if you prepare your body early. Be ready to bunt as soon as the pitcher makes a move. As long as you execute the bunt properly, your goal of moving the runner will be accomplished.

Bunting begins before the hitter even steps into the batter's box. You receive the sign, and before you step into the batter's box, you must mentally prepare to bunt. According to Garth Iorg of the Toronto Blue Jays organization, "Bunting is an attitude; you gotta want to bunt."

Move up in the box so you're closer to the pitcher before your bunt. Because the field is square, you have more space to work with at the front of the box. Here, in front of home plate, the bat will start in fair territory. A ball bouncing left or right can stay fair more easily with this additional space. Standing deep in the box narrows your field, as shown in the diagram.

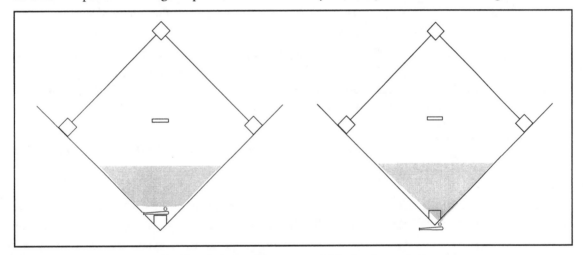

Moving up in the box offers you more fair territory for your bunt.

MAC FACT: *To bunt, move up in the box and increase your work area.*

You will initiate the pivot bunt by stepping up and in towards the front inside corner of the batter's box. For a right-handed hitter, this means a jab step towards the second baseman; left-handed hitters will step towards the shortstop. This step will give you a better chance of covering the outside portion of the strike zone when you are trying to bunt. Unlike back side rotational hitting, when you attempt to bunt, shift your weight to the front foot as you step up and in, and at the same time use a back foot pivot to turn your body around to face the pitcher.

After completing the pivot, your toes are facing the pitcher. You should be in an athletic position, able to move in any direction, with your weight on the balls of your feet. Your knees

An athletic bunting position.

Use your knees to move down to the ball while keeping your arms and bat still.

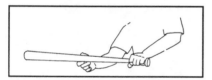

Pinch the bat between your thumb and forefinger.

are flexed, ready to serve as a springboard, the bend varying according to your comfort level. You may find it easier to see the ball if you crouch lower than your normal hitting stance. Or, you may want to keep your eyes on the same consistent plane whether you are bunting or hitting.

Knees are crucial to the bunting procedure. Knees control the lateral movement of your body. Keep your hands and arms still, and use your knees to move up and down to the ball.

MAC FACT: *Use your knees to position your body to bunt.*

Your top hand should slide up the bat approximately five inches. Pinch the bat between your thumb and the side of the forefinger. Finger placement is important for avoiding injuries. Don't wrap your fingers around the bat because if you misread the pitch or the ball tails in late, you may break the exposed fingers.

MAC FACT: *Pinch the bat between the thumb and side of the forefinger.*

In bunting, get the barrel of the bat as far out in front as possible. This position will help you see the ball connect You want your arms to be flexed at the elbow and extended. The top hand will serve as an anchor on the bat, ensuring solid contact. The bottom hand acts as a rudder, angling the bat in order to steer the ball to the desired side of the infield.

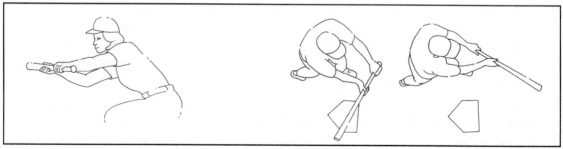

Extend your hands and the barrel of the bat out in front of your body.

Angle the bat to steer the ball to the desired location.

Start the barrel of the bat at the top of the strike zone. If the throw is above the bat, the pitch is a ball — don't bunt.

MAC FACT: *Only bunt strikes!*

Now is when your knees come in to play. If the ball is below the bat, your knees will lower the body, and therefore the barrel of the bat, to the level of contact. It's important to minimize hand movement because it jerks the bat uncontrollably as the ball approaches, causing you to foul off good bunting pitches. Lowering the body and the bat by way of bending the knees is a smoother approach to a successful bunt.

MAC FACT: *Keep your hands still when bunting!*

Always keep the barrel of the bat at a height greater than your hands. Many hitters drop the barrel of the bat to bunt a low pitch. Dropping the barrel reduces the amount of surface area available. At this angle, there is less opportunity to make solid contact because very little of the bat is on the same plane as the incoming pitch. With the barrel above the hands, however, the bat is level and has a larger surface area for contact.

MAC FACT: *Keep the barrel above your hands.*

Start the barrel of the bat at the top of the strike zone (top). Do not drop the barrel of the bat (bottom) — it reduces the surface area of the bat.

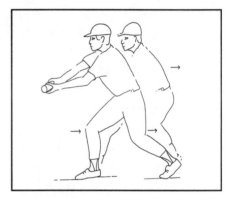

Rock your body back to cushion and deaden the ball.

As the pitch approaches, keep your eye on the ball and watch it hit the bat. Again, keep your hands still, and let the ball do the work, as if trying to catch the ball with the end of the bat. Some coaches teach their hitters to cradle the ball with the bat. By cradling the ball, you reduce the bounce, avoiding a line drive back to the pitcher. Explore the pros and cons of each method for yourself.

One major league organization encourages hitters to rock their body back when making contact, letting the knees control the action. As contact is made, your knees will shift your body back slightly, deadening the ball on impact. The rocking movement seems more effective than cradling the ball simply because it enables the hands to remain still.

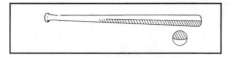

Bunt the top half of the ball
with the bottom half of the bat.

When bunting, make contact with the top half of the ball using the bottom half of the barrel of the bat in order to get the ball on the ground. Hitting the bottom half of the ball results in pop-ups.

MAC FACT: *Bunt the top half of the ball.*

In sacrifice bunts, concentrate on keeping the ball away from the pitcher. Remember, bunts to the third base side of the infield force the third baseman to make a longer throw, increasing the chance of error. When the pitcher is left-handed, bunting down the first baseline is more likely to result in a base hit, since left-handers fall to the other side of the mound, making it difficult to retrieve the ball and make the play.

In summary, the following are key to the sacrifice bunt:
- move up in the box
- step up and in
- pivot and shift your weight forward
- stay on the balls of your feet
- slide the top hand up the bat
- get the barrel out in front of the body
- flex knees and elbows
- bunt only strikes
- start the bat at the top of the strike zone
- use the knees to adjust down
- keep the barrel above the hands
- bunt the top half of the ball
- rock your weight back at contact to deaden the ball

RIGHT-HANDED BUNTING FOR A HIT

Bunting for a hit can be an added dimension to the offensive talents of a player and team. If your team is struggling against a certain pitcher, bunting for a hit might provide the spark the team needs to rally. If you're in a personal slump, the bunt might end it. In the scorebook, a hit is a hit. No one remembers whether it was a line drive or an infield squibbler.

A bunt fails when it's tapped right back to the pitcher — a sure out. A foul ball isn't so bad because you have another chance to hit. Again, bunt down the third baseline. Bunting the ball along the baselines is achieved by obtaining a good bat angle. Rather than positioning the bat so that it's square to the pitcher, square it to the baseline that you're bunting along.

MAC FACT: *Get a good bat angle when bunting for a hit; a foul ball is better than an out.*

To bunt for a hit, find the most comfortable stance. Right-handed bunters can do the drag bunt which is achieved by dropping back your right (back) foot. As you drop your back foot, pull back your left elbow and extend the top hand arm out in front of your body. This will accomplish a good bat angle, square to the third base side of the infield.

The second method of drag bunting involves a different lower body movement. Take a jab step with your front foot, then pull back the left elbow to get the bat around. The jab step is very short, about four inches, on an angle towards the second baseman.

There are advantages to each method, so use the comfort factor to determine which method you use. The drop step is easier to read by opposing fielders. The jab step, while more deceptive, makes you susceptible to inside pitches. In both cases, be sure to get the bat out in front of your body.

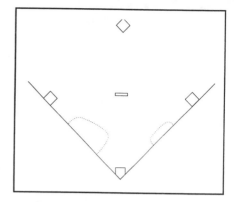

Desired locations when bunting for a hit.

Drop your back foot ...

LEFT-HANDED BUNTING FOR A HIT

As a left-handed hitter, you have a definite advantage when bunting for a hit because you can hide your intentions until the last possible moment. You can also have increased success using both sides of the infield. Most importantly, you're a step closer to first base — a big advantage on close plays.

... or take a jab step with your front foot.

Initiate the bunt by lifting the back foot (left) and crossing it over in front, stepping towards the shortstop. This will prevent you from running before getting the bunt down. The biggest mistake with left-handed bunters is the inability to stay on the plate until contact is made.

Crossover and stop; keep your body under control.

MAC FACT: *Stay on the plate until contact is made — don't leave too early.*

Like right-handers, you must achieve a good bat angle. The last thing you want to do is bunt the ball straight back to the pitcher. The body must be stopped and under control before you make contact. For this reason, this method of bunting for a hit is referred to as "stop action." Too much movement can lead to pop-ups or foul balls as your body is not ready to bunt. Remember that the location of the bunt is more important than the surprise factor. If no one expects you to bunt, but the ball is tapped back to the pitcher, you are still out. A well-placed bunt, on the other hand, is difficult to catch regardless of the defense.

OVERVIEW

As a coach, understand how to properly implement bunting into practice sessions. It's imperative that you discourage players from simply going through the motions in practice. This will catch up with the team and player on game day.

Set up a separate bunting station during your workout. This station can be located behind the backstop or in the outfield. Don't use your entire infield to work on bunting alone. Incorporate it into batting drills without disrupting the flow of practice. Monitor the bunting station to ensure correct mechanics and good work habits. Try instituting one of the bunting drills, then have players bunt in live situations.

One of the secrets to genuine bunting situations during practice is maintaining consistency in pitch velocity. Pitches should be like those expected in an actual game. Use a pitching machine or cut down on the distance of the throw to prepare players for game-like conditions and ball velocity.

BUNTING DRILLS

#1 — THE BUNTING STICK DRILL

Objective: To receive the ball with the bat.

Setup: Cut off the last eight inches of the top or barrel of a wooden bat and attach a lacrosse stick pocket to the end. Or use a lacrosse stick for the drill, making sure it's not too long.

Procedure: Try to catch the ball in the netting. Rock back to receive the ball.

Coach's Note: Check for proper grip. Stress the proper mechanics throughout the drill. Bunt strikes only. Balls should be thrown at half distance or game-like velocity.

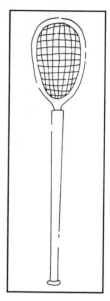

Bunting Stick

#2 — GLOVE ON BAT DRILL

Objective: To receive the ball with the bat.

Setup: Place your glove on the end of the bat.

Procedure: As with the bunting stick, attempt to receive the ball in the glove. Rock back to catch the ball.

Coach's Note: Check for proper grip. Stress the proper mechanics throughout the drill. Bunt strikes only. Balls should be thrown at half distance or game-like velocity.

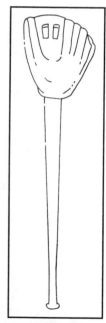

Glove on Bat Drill

#3 — HALF BAT DRILL

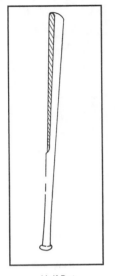

Half Bat

Objective: To practice bunting the top half of the ball with the bottom half of the bat.

Setup: Cut the barrel of the bat in half down to the handle.

Procedure: Hold the bat with the flat side facing the sky. You have only the bottom half of the barrel of the bat to make contact. Concentrate on bunting the top half of the ball. You're using half of a bat to bunt the ball.

Coach's Note: Start with slower pitches until the hitter gets accustomed to the smaller surface area on the bat.

#4 — ONE-HANDED BUNTING DRILL

Objective: To use the top hand as an anchor.
To develop good bat control.

Setup: Designate an area where players can practice bunting. This might be on the field, in the outfield, or behind the backstop. A pitcher is needed with a bucket of balls.

One-handed Bunting Drill

Procedure: Grip the bat with your top hand. This hand will slide up the bat several inches. As the pitcher delivers the ball, try to bunt with only one hand (top hand) on the bat.

Coach's Note: Make sure the arm is extended out in front. The hitter must keep her eyes focused on the ball.

#5 — THE BUNTING GAME

Objective: To practice bunting for a hit.
To control the location of the bunt.

Setup: Use ropes or a mat to set up target areas along the third baseline. Use a few different targets, but one large area will suffice.

Procedure: Set the number of bunt attempts yourself. Points are awarded for bunts which land in certain target areas. The best location receives the highest points; bunts missing target area earn zero points.

Coach's Note: Establish an award system for top bunting players or groups of players. They can compete individually or in small groups.

Variation: Several hula hoops may also serve as target areas. However, the tubing on the hoop may prevent balls from actually entering the circle.

SEVENTH INNING
BASERUNNING

BASERUNNING

Baserunning may be the most overlooked aspect in baseball today. And yet, it's as important as hitting or throwing. To practice baserunning, you don't even need a diamond. You can hone your baserunning skills in a gymnasium or even an empty field.

Good baserunning puts pressure on the defence, generates extra bases, and produces runs almost every game. On the other hand, poor baserunning can cost you bases and limit your offensive performances. Listen to what Ron Polk, Head Coach of Mississippi State University, has to say about this facet of the game:

> *Baserunning might be one of the most neglected areas of baseball taught on all levels, from youth leagues all the way up to major leagues. Since baseball games are won or lost many times on the base paths, a coach needs to spend plenty of time in practice perfecting baserunning skills... A team that has an aggressive baserunning game can have a devastating effect on a defense, causing them to make errors on even routine plays. The coach who can prepare his players to run the bases effectively, will find that his club can take advantage of defensive mistakes much quicker.*
>
> — Ron Polk, *Baseball Playbook*

Please don't confuse baserunning skills with speed. Speed is a god-given talent that some athletes possess, and not every player on your squad will be so blessed. Nonetheless, every one of your players can become effective base runners if they pay attention and practice the skills.

Remember this phrase: "disciplined aggression." Be aggressive on the bases, always looking for the opportunity to take an extra base or capitalize on a defensive miscue. At the same time, exercise discipline and care so that your aggressive move doesn't turn into an advantage for the other team.

Consider the following scenario from a tournament championship between Brock University, where I was Head Coach, and a college from New York State. We had a one-run game in the fourth inning. The bases were loaded with one of our fastest runners at the plate and above average speed runners on the bases. The hitter beat the pitch into the ground and the ball bounced high in the air to the second baseman, who was playing in to cut the run off at the plate. The player waited for the ball to come down, then made a hurried throw to the plate. The ball was thrown wild past the catcher. The runner at second made an aggressive turn at third and I sent him home as the catcher raced to the backstop. The only way this runner stood a chance was due to the fact that an "aggressive turn" was part of his daily practice regimen. He beat the throw to the plate; however, the play wasn't over. The hitter also made an aggressive turn at first base and continued for second. The pitcher, who received the throw from the catcher at home plate, turned and threw to second base. Immediately after the ball was released, I sent the runner from third, who started the play at first base, to score easily. The shortstop stepped in front of the bag to take the throw and wheeled to the plate but was too late. The hitter continued on to third base.

The entire play was both amazing, and confusing. In one short chopper, we cleared the bases and left the hitter at third base. What makes the play astounding is the fact that there was only one error — the original wild toss to the plate that probably would not have gotten an out anyway. That play took the steam right out of our opponent. They could not rebound and we coasted to victory. In my opinion, our daily dedication to baserunning made the play possible. Every one of the players involved were committed to "disciplined aggression" on the bases. They had good jumps and took aggressive turns. It clearly made the difference on this occasion.

RUNNING FROM HOME TO FIRST

Running from home to first base involves certain mental and physical acts which occur on any ground ball hit in the infield. If the ball gets through the infield, then you must change your physical and mental approach. On balls which remain in the infield, the key is to get out of the batter's box quickly.

Here are seven steps to running for first base:

i) Keep your head and eyes on the ball as you make contact without, however, watching where it goes.

ii) Your back foot should be carrying most of your weight; it should leave the batter's box first in a crossover step.

iii) After three steps, "sneak a peek" to see if the ball remained in the infield or if it got through. Sneaking a peak means a glance, not a complete head turn, which would slow you down.

iv) At this point, you're committed to first base, so focus on it. As you approach first base, hit the front part of the bag. It makes no difference which foot hits the bag as long as you don't slow down. Hitting the front part of the bag is possible if you focus on it as early as possible. I believe that if you concentrate on the front part, your feet will naturally work out so that you do not have to break stride.

v) Don't lunge at the base; run through it.

vi) As soon as you hit the bag, turn your head and look to the right. You are looking to see if there is an overthrow. If the ball is thrown away, you can immediately change your route and head to second base.

vii) Finally, you will break, and slow down.

This slowing is called "breaking down." As you cross the base, you should be straddling the baseline, without veering left or right. Many young players incorrectly assume that they must veer off to the right in foul territory. This turn is not only unnecessary, it hinders your ability to take another base on an overthrow. The "break down" process requires you to spread your feet wider apart (side-to-side) and lower your centre of gravity. In doing so, you will take short choppy strides. This action will allow you to slow down and gain control.

Remember your goal of developing muscle memory. Constant repetition and reinforcement of these principles is necessary for effective baserunning to become automatic.

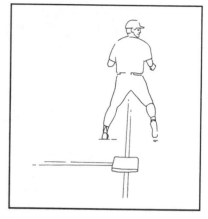

After reaching first base, break down with short, choppy strides and look right.

HOME AROUND FIRST

You will round first base on any ball hit to the outfield, or on ground balls penetrating the infield. On fly balls, your mental commitment to rounding first base occurs immediately. On ground balls, this commitment can't happen until you've "sneaked a peek" and watched the ball into the outfield.

In these situations, the approach to leaving the box is the same as running from home to first. Keep your head and eyes on the ball at contact and avoid watching its journey. Leave the box with your back foot initiating a crossover step.

The moment you determine the ball is in the outfield, the mental and physical approach to baserunning changes. Your

After contact, your back foot will leave the box first.

prime target is now second base. Take a route which follows a straight line between first and second base. Focus on a point about 8 feet off the baseline in foul territory. Run in a straight line to this target and make your turn to first base. This "point of turning route," will differ for each player and age group. The coach's goal is to help each player find a good route not too far from the baseline, but which enables them to move in a straight line to the next base.

MAC FACT: *Round the base by heading into foul territory and creating a straight line from that base to the next.*

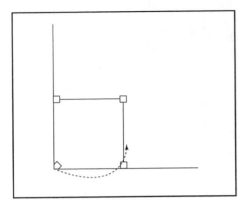

When rounding the base, make a turn which allows you to head in a straight line to the next base.

Push off the inside corner of the bag.

As you approach first base, make contact on the inside corner of the bag. Ideally, you'd like the right foot to make contact. However, making this a baserunning objective will only serve to slow you down if you must break stride in order to hit the bag with your right foot. It's more important for you to avoid breaking stride and succeed in hitting the inside corner. As you hit the base, you should push off the corner to generate some speed. The ball of your foot should hit the infield side and use the base as a catapult.

MAC FACT: *Hit the inside corner of the base with either foot, and push off.*

The moment you know first base will not be challenged, think about second. Direct all your energy to taking an aggressive route to the next base. Every player must take an "aggressive turn." An aggressive turn is when you continue to run to the next base, stopping only when the outfielder fields the ball cleanly and gets it back to the infield quickly. When this happens, retreat quickly to the base you just touched. Even on routine singles, take an aggressive turn in case the outfielder bobbles the ball or makes a lazy throw to the infield. An aggressive turn involves a total commitment to the next base and forcing the outfielder to make you stop. You are thinking about the next base until then.

MAC FACT: *Always take aggressive turns and force the outfielder to stop the base runner.*

The length of your turn will be determined by the location of the ball. If the ball is fielded by the left fielder, then you can wander a long way from first base before you have to stop because it will take a very long throw to get you out at first base. Left fielders will not attempt such a throw. But, in the meantime, you're forcing him to make a good throw to second base. If the centre fielder fields the ball, reduce the distance of your turn around first base by a few steps because she is closer to you. Similarly, shorten your turn on balls hit to right field because she could potentially throw you out. In any event, never compromise an aggressive turn. Rather, be cautious of the distance depending on which fielder picks up the ball.

Throw on the brakes once the fielder forces you to stop. Stop the same way you would when running to first base — by breaking down. Spread your feet wider apart, and take short choppy strides, never taking your eyes off the ball. As you slow down, watch the fielder and return to first base. This breaking down process will occur directly on the baseline. Remember that your goal is to take a straight line from first base to second. During the turning phase you'll make a decision about taking an extra base. Thus you want to be in the best position possible when you make that decision. If you make a wide turn and then head for second and get thrown out on a bang-bang play, your turn and route may be to blame. If you took a more direct route, you would have saved two or three steps and perhaps slid into second safely. In summary, shorten the distance between first and second by taking a wider turn before first base.

MAC FACT: *When making a turn, you should try to take a straight line to the base where there is a potential play.*

Although I teach the same turn on any ball hit to the outfield (only the distance is altered according to the location of the batted ball), I recently acquired an interesting coaching tip on balls hit to the left fielder. Garth Iorg of the Toronto Blue Jays suggests that you run almost directly at first base, and then take a wide turn and line up yourself, second base, and the left fielder. When doing so, an aggressive turn covering significant distance is necessary and easily achieved because you're dealing with the left fielder. From this vantage point, you can observe the throw. If you see that the throw is not on target, you can continue to second base. If, however, an accurate throw is made, retreat to first.

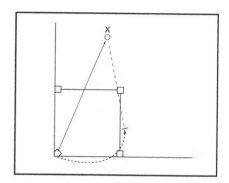

An advanced baserunning technique: on balls hit to left, line up yourself, the base and the outfielder in order to capitalize on potential errant throws.

Iorg's theory is that you can observe the throw only if you are lined up with the base and the fielder. There's merit to this concept, and it could be applied at the older levels with intelligent base runners. If you took a turn which positioned you in a straight line between first and second base, you might not recognize the line of the throw and thus miss out on opportunities that are caused by errant tosses.

ROUNDING OTHER BASES

The concept of aggressive turns isn't limited to first base. Base runners should take aggressive turns at each and every base the moment you know it's safe to do so.

Heading from first to third base, take a wide turn before second base so you'll be positioned in a straight line as you push off the bag and head for third. As you start your turn, your eyes should be focused on the coach in the third base coaching box, who can see the play in front of him, while you're too busy watching your route. Don't watch the ball. Rely on the coach to make decisions. Again, watching the ball just slows you down.

MAC FACT: *When running first to third, pay attention to the third base coach, not the ball.*

When trying to score from second base, you must pick up your coach's signal immediately. You should round third base so that you're on a direct route from third to home. An aggressive turn is mandatory because the coach may not make his or her decision whether or not to send you home until you are part of the way down the baseline.

Regardless of your intended base, a banana turn before the base will put you on a direct course to the next. Round each base with an aggressive turn. Don't assume that the ball will be caught or that the fielder will make a good throw. Force the defence to react to your running game.

PRIMARY LEADOFFS

A primary lead is the initial distance you can get off the base while the pitcher still has the baseball on the mound. It is the standard or first leadoff that you can take. Primary leads differ depending on which base you're on.

When leading off first base, you need a consistent method for getting a good primary lead. An efficient leadoff is where you can return safely in the event of a pickoff attempt by the pitcher, yet still gain enough ground to potentially steal the next base. While there are many ways of securing this lead, you must be cautious.

When establishing a primary lead, walk off with your left foot and then turn in to the pitcher.

Your eyes must never leave the pitcher. If you turn your head, even for a short time, it might give the pitcher an edge to pick you off. A similar result may happen if you're looking at the ground. You must get this lead without checking your distance. Also, you should take this lead from the inside corner of first base. Leaving from this corner will create the impression that the lead is not very big and so the pitcher may not pay much attention. Finally, while moving out to the leadoff position, avoid crossing over your feet. If the pitcher makes a throw at that moment, your feet will get tangled up during your scramble to return to first. Instead, use shuffle steps.

MAC FACT: *When leading off, never take your eyes off the pitcher.*

The standard leadoff distance against a right-handed pitcher is the length of your body with outstretched arms, plus one step. This lead will enable you to push off and dive back safely to first base. Against left-handed pitchers, however, eliminate the extra step. A leftie can throw over quicker and you want to avoid giving up unnecessary outs due to pickoffs.

One method of taking a primary leadoff is by starting with both heels on the bag and facing second base. Walk off the base with your left foot first, followed by the right one. As the right foot lands, turn your body in so that it faces the hitting area. Remember, always keep your eyes on the pitcher. From this spot, you should take one large shuffle step. This distance should equal your height with outstretched arms.

Or, take three and a half shuffle steps. A shuffle step means stepping towards second base with the right foot and then taking the left foot to the same spot as the right one. The foot closest to the base will replace the other foot as you move away from first base. The toes will be pointing towards home plate during these shuffle steps.

Coaches should take each player and have them lie down and reach for first base. You need to mark the spot where your feet last touched the ground. Once you've established the distance, you should discover your own method of getting to that spot. Your system doesn't matter so long as you can get to the same spot every time without taking your eyes off the pitcher. Memorize your lead by practicing it.

If the pitcher throws to first, cross over with your right foot and dive back to first base. When diving back, use your right hand to reach for the back corner of the base. This spot forces the first baseman to make a longer tag and leaves a smaller portion of your body to touch. Turn your head during the dive so that you are looking into foul territory. This serves a dual purpose. First, it protects your face from the ball. Second, you can take advantage of any wild throws.

When leading off from second base, a measurable leadoff is not as important. There's no defensive player stationed directly on the bag, which

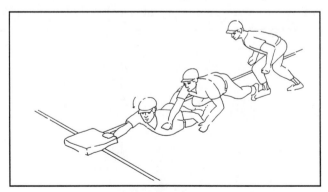

If a pickoff attempt is made, cross over and drive back to the outside corner of the base with your left hand.

enables you to cover more ground. Rely on verbal assistance from one of your coaches. They should be helping you to either take extra steps or reduce your lead. As with first base, your goal is to watch the pitcher at all times. You can't get picked off unless the pitcher throws the ball, so it only makes sense that you should watch the pitcher constantly.

If there's a potential force play at third base, your lead should be right on the baseline. Take the shortest route possible for any force play. If you're in the position to score from second on a base hit, the lead from second should be about 3 feet behind the baseline. This lead will establish a narrower turn at third base and a more direct or straight route to home plate.

SECONDARY LEADS

The secondary lead is crucial. Secondary lead refers to the movement which occurs once the pitcher has committed himself to delivering the ball to home plate. In other words, after you've taken your first, or primary lead, you must then take a secondary lead.

The secondary lead allows you to generate good momentum towards the next base, in case contact is made. If the ball is hit on the ground, you might have a chance to beat the throw. Or, on balls hit into the outfield, you might take an extra base simply because of the additional ground covered during your secondary phase of the leadoff.

MAC FACT: *A secondary lead shortens the distance to the next base.*

A secondary leadoff is achieved by taking two big shuffle steps once the pitcher delivers the ball. Gain maximum distance on each shuffle step, covering as much ground as possible in a controlled manner. On a regular-size diamond, you should end up 15 to 20 feet away from the base you started at. Watch the ball at all times. As the ball passes through the hitting zone, you will be coming down from the second shuffle step. From this position, you have two choices.

Two large shuffle steps make up a proper secondary lead.

You can pivot on your left foot and hustle back to first base because the catcher caught the ball. Or, pivot on your right foot and crossover to start running to the next base because the catcher missed the ball or it was put into play.

MAC FACT: *The secondary lead is accomplished by taking two powerful shuffle steps.*

Secondary leads are extremely important to the overall running game. They put more pressure on the defence and permit the offensive team to take extra bases. They also eat up distance between two bases. However, they do require your attention. If you drop your head or return to the base in a lackadaisical manner, then you may be picked off by the catcher.

STEALING BASES

When a known base stealer reaches first base, the game of baseball witnesses one of the most enjoyable confrontations. Everyone in the ballpark may know that the player is going to attempt to steal. Yet, the fun comes in trying to determine which pitch will bring the dramatic moment. That guessing game is part of the preparation the defensive team will use to thwart any stolen base attempts. Similarly, the offensive player must prepare him or herself to gain as much of an advantage as possible.

Study the opposing pitcher for the distinguishing feature that she shows when delivering the ball to the plate, every pitcher differs. For example, one pitcher may move her shoulders first when she is about to deliver to the plate. Another pitcher may move her feet first. In any event, you must discover this feature prior to getting to first base. Don't wait until you're on base to look for the pitcher's first movement. Once on base, you want to apply what you have already learned.

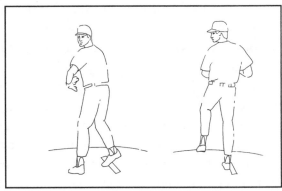

Watch the right-handed pitcher's heels; they will indicate his intentions.

When attempting to steal off a right-hander, you should watch the pitcher's heels. If the back heel (the one touching the rubber) moves first, the pitcher is throwing over to first. If her front or lead heel moves first, then the pitcher is committed to the plate.

MAC FACT: *Watch the heels of a right-handed pitcher to determine when she is throwing over to first or delivering the ball.*

Read left-handed pitchers by observing their shoulders.

Reading left-handed pitchers is a much more difficult task. Quite often, you are trying to read his move to first base, and not look for the movement of commitment to the plate. Runners tend to read lefties opposite of a right-handed pitcher. With right-handers you try to determine when they're going to throw home. With left-handers, try to learn his move to first base. Left-handers can be deceptive. In general, watch the pitcher's shoulders. In order for a left-hander to throw to first base, he must turn his shoulders. You will notice that his back shoulder will begin to turn and the front shoulder will follow and end up pointing towards you. This shoulder turn is essential for the throwing process. When he goes to the plate, this shoulder turn is not needed because his shoulders have already established the direction needed to throw.

MAC FACT: *Watch the shoulders of a left-handed pitcher in order to read his move to first base.*

There are other factors which will give you an advantage and increase your chances of successfully stealing a base. If possible, try to get a walking lead. A walking lead is obtained as you move away from the base in a standard walking motion. You're not measuring this leadoff, nor are you trying to stop. Attempt to keep the body moving. This momentum can generate a very good jump or first step en route to the next base. Obtaining a walking lead is not easy. Occasionally, however, the pitcher is not paying attention and he may not force you to stop. If he doesn't stop you, you can keep the feet moving and get some momentum going early.

In most steal situations from first base, the runner will not be able to keep his feet moving by way of a walking lead. Only when they know they're going to steal should runners open up and stagger their lead foot so that the toes are pointing in the direction of third base. This action of opening up the lead foot will give you a chance to get a better jump.

Your footwork is started by a pivot-crossover step, which has been discussed in previous sections of this book. Your lead foot (the one closest to second base) will pivot so that your toes are pointed at second base and the right foot will cross over to start the running process.

When stealing, use the pivot-crossover step.

Avoid standing straight up to run. If you start in a crouched position, you should explode from that point and stay low. Not until you have taken three or four steps should the body have raised to near full height. The body will come up gradually after covering some distance, similar to the takeoff of an airplane.

MAC FACT: *Stay low and explode; don't straighten up to run.*

Even if you can't get a walking lead, you should generate some momentum when you're going to steal. Physics teaches that an object in motion is more mobile if it stays in motion. Potential base-stealers should take note. It's very difficult to get a good jump if you've come to a complete stop. Your movement might be a slight rocking action on the balls of the feet. The problem with this movement is that you're not in a good position to steal if you're rocking back towards first base. Keep in mind that any rocking action is a slight movement and not noticeable to the pitcher. Another type of movement which you may apply is a slight bounce on alternate feet. In other words, you will raise one heel slightly, and then raise the other heel. Coaches should make suggestions and information available to players, and let comfort and their athletic ability take over. It doesn't matter how the movement is done, so long as you keep the body in motion in anticipation of a good jump.

MAC FACT: *When stealing bases, get your body into motion early in order to get a quicker jump.*

Don't attempt to steal third unless you've got a walking lead. Middle infielders will be trying to fill the infield holes while keeping you close to the base. Your leadoff should be directly on the baseline. Leading off behind the baseline lengthens the distance to the next base.

MAC FACT: *A walking leadoff is essential to steal third base.*

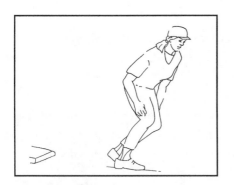
Use a walking lead to steal third base.

When stealing third base, start your walking lead with the body angled and facing third base. This lets you get to proper running form immediately. If you start while facing the pitcher, you'll lose time because you must turn yourself around before beginning your run.

Try to get a good distance from second base before you start for third. If the pitcher interrupts your run, take a large shuffle step back to second and then continue with the walking lead so you're in constant motion.

In order to successfully steal a base you must be sure to get a good jump, covering as much ground as possible between second and third in a very short time. You must do this as soon as the pitcher commits to the throw. If you hesitate, or get a late jump, cancel your steal and wait for another opportunity. Attempting a stolen base simply because the coach gives the signal isn't always a wise decision. As a coach, remind players that there will be occasions when cancelling the planned steal is necessary. This is always better than running into an easy out.

MAC FACT: *Get a good jump before you steal.*

The delayed steal can be an effective offensive tool when you're facing a lazy catcher, a left-hander with a good pickoff move, or when you need to get a player of average speed to second base. When successful, the delay can provide both an offensive and mental boost to the team.

Timing and preparation are essential for determining when to use the delayed steal. Watch the opposing catcher. With runners on base, does she have a habit of going to her knees to throw the ball back to the pitcher? A catcher with this habit is very vulnerable to the delay. Also, observe the actions of the middle infielders. With a runner on first, one of them should take a few steps towards second base on every pitch that gets through to the catcher. If they're not breaking for the bag, they're susceptible to delay because it's possible no one will get to second base in time to receive the catcher's throw.

MAC FACT: *Watch your opposition's defense to see if a delayed steal is a good strategy.*

When attempting a delayed steal, avoid drawing attention to yourself. Take a normal primary lead followed by a secondary lead of two shuffle steps. The delayed steal begins once your right foot lands on the second shuffle step. As your foot comes down, pivot and cross over to take off for second base.

MAC FACT: *The delayed steal is performed by running for second base only after taking your secondary lead.*

Accomplish a straight steal of second by taking a primary lead and leaving the moment the pitcher is committed to throwing home. The delayed steal, on the other hand, includes a primary lead followed by a secondary lead, and then running for second after a slight pause. With the delayed steal, you're trying to take an additional base by using the element of surprise.

RUNNING FROM THIRD BASE

When you reach third base, you must approach baserunning differently. First of all, the primary lead at third isn't useful because you can't go anywhere until the pitcher starts the action, and putting distance between yourself and the bag isn't vital at third. To try for a large leadoff from third also risks being picked off by the pitcher, so stay put.

The primary lead from third must be taken in foul territory. If you are struck by a fair ball, you are automatically out. If the ball is put in play by the hitter, it is essential that you are located in foul territory.

MAC FACT: *The primary leadoff from third base must be in foul territory.*

While the primary lead is insignificant, your secondary leadoff is the top priority when on third base. You must generate optimum distance and momentum heading towards home plate. Start your secondary lead as the pitcher delivers the ball. During the secondary lead, get your body moving in a positive direction towards home in anticipation of a passed ball or wild pitch.

MAC FACT: *A secondary lead with the body moving towards home plate is the objective when running from third base.*

Nothing is more frustrating than a runner who takes a huge lead, starts sprinting down the line only to throw on the brakes and start returning to third before the ball has even arrived at the plate. In this scenario, if the ball gets away from the catcher, you're in no position to score when heading back to third. The goal at third base is to establish good momentum towards the plate.

If the pitcher starts in a full windup, begin your secondary leadoff after the pitcher lifts his leg. If the pitcher starts from the stretch position, start your secondary lead when he commits to the plate. Avoid starting the secondary too soon because you may be too far down the line, or forced to put on the brakes. The secondary leadoff is a controlled trot, not a sprint. Similar to the lead from second base, start with your body facing the direction you want to run. Rather than the shuffle method, use normal running form and jog in a controlled manner. Good momentum from third can allow you to score on a ball in the dirt, even if it lands relatively close to the catcher.

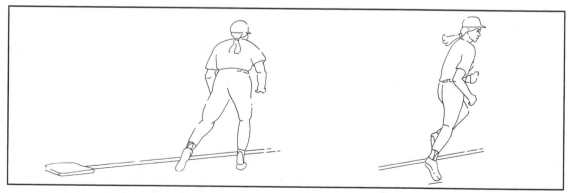

When leading off of third base, your body should face home plate. You should move in a controlled jog or trot.

Don't stop moving forward until the catcher receives the ball. Work on your timing so that you can continue moving right up to the point when the ball is caught, without being too far down the line. Starting the secondary lead too late is more favourable than moving too early when running from third base. If the ball is caught, you'll return to third base in fair territory. Coming back to the bag in fair territory provides the catcher with an obstacle if she wants to attempt a pickoff.

MAC FACT: *Return to third base in fair territory to make it difficult for the catcher to attempt a pickoff play.*

Running from third base will vary with the style of hitter at the plate. If a right-handed hitter is up, you can take an extra step and cover more distance because the catcher would have a difficult time on any pickoff attempt. With a left-handed hitter up, the catcher has a clear line of vision and no obstacle to avoid in the event of a pickoff.

TAGGING UP TO SCORE ON A FLY BALL

On any fly ball, you must automatically return to third base. Even if the ball seems to be heading for the gap or over the fielder's head, you must return to the base. If the ball does fall in for a hit, you can still score easily. If, however, the ball is caught and you have started for home, you might not have enough time to return to third to tag up and score.

While the coach decides whether you run on a fly ball, you decide when to begin the run. Once the ball is airborne, the coach signals that you will run. You position yourself to see the ball and then run once it's caught. Don't wait for the coach to tell you when to begin. This just slows you down and confuses things. Glance to see the ball while your body faces home plate.

 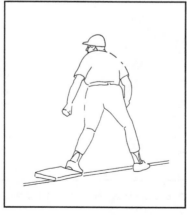

Your right foot will be on the base when tagging up on flyballs down the left field line (left). On balls hit to the other parts of the outfield, tag up with your left foot on the base (right).

MAC FACT: *Keep your eye on the ball when you are deciding when to run.*

If the ball is hit in foul territory down the third base line, place your right foot on the bag and look over your right shoulder. If the ball is hit to another field, get your left foot on the bag and look over your left shoulder. Your shoulder glance dictates which foot should be on the bag. If foot and shoulder are the same, it's easier to watch the ball and prepare to run.

MAC FACT: *Assume the running position, then glance over your shoulder to see the ball.*

It is important that you position your body so that it faces the direction in which you are headed. Push off with the ball of your foot from the side of third base facing home plate. This will provide you with momentum and thrust for the dash home.

ANTICIPATING BALLS IN THE DIRT

Watch for balls that head into the dirt after a pitch, then take off immediately for the next base. If the ball is thrown into the dirt, the catcher has to block the ball, scramble to pick it up, and then make an accurate throw to second base. If you begin your dash as soon as you see the play forming, he will not have time to throw you out.

MAC FACT: *Start for the next base as soon as you read that the ball is headed into the dirt.*

Occasionally, the ball will skip straight into the catcher's mitt and you become an easy out. The chances of this type of hop are very rare, and I would applaud any runner who correctly reads the ball in the dirt, but is thrown out on a flukey play.

There are two ways to successfully read balls in the dirt. Watch the flight of the ball, or watch the catcher. If the catcher drops to her knees, she is committing herself to blocking the ball, and you can head to the next base. When watching the flight of the ball, run as soon as you see that the pitch will hit the ground before it can be caught.

MAC FACT: *You can read the pitch in the dirt by watching either the ball or the catcher.*

BASERUNNING DRILLS

In baserunning, coaches should ensure that practice conditions are similar to those expected during the intensity of an actual game.

Here are two ways to practice baserunning skills: Batting Practice (BP) Baserunning, and Baserunning Circuits. Within the sample plans listed below you'll find ample room for flexibility and variation. Modify the circuits to work on other baserunning skills, according to your needs for that day. Replace some of my stations with drills which meet your own baserunning goals.

#1 — RUNNING THE PROPER ROUTES

Objective: To ensure that players take the most direct route to the base.

Setup: Use gloves, helmets, or cones to plan several running paths. Portable or throw-down bases are also available to set up routes.

Procedure: To practice the proper turn at first base, take a dry swing and then start running, staying within the established path.

Coach's Note: Check to see that the other components of good baserunning are still adhered to.

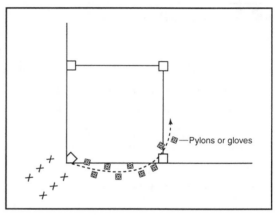

Running The Proper Routes

#2 — BP BASERUNNING DRILLS

Objective: To practice different baserunning situations in a game-like atmosphere.
To react to the ball leaving the bat.

Setup: Form three groups for batting practice. One group will be hitting, one will be fielding balls, and the third will be running the bases, wearing helmets.

Procedure: Runners start at home plate and, one at a time, react to the pitch. If the batter hits a ground ball to shortstop, run to first in proper fashion. From first base, take the proper leadoff, and react to the next pitch. Treat each pitch as you would in an actual game.

Coach's Note: If possible, have a coach working strictly with the running group. This coach can make sure that the players are practicing at full speed. Because batting practice pitchers usually try to throw in rapid succession, it may be impossible for players to react to each and every pitch. It's important that they treat the drill properly even if it means allowing some pitches to go by.

Variation: You may wish to modify the BP baserunning by having every player attempt to steal third once they get to second base, or by attempting a hit and run. In either case, they would be reacting to the pitch instead of waiting for contact.

#3 — BASERUNNING CIRCUIT I

Objective: To practice reading the pitcher's movements.

Setup: Four pitchers are at the mound, facing a base. They each set up as if the base they are facing is home plate. Runners are situated at each of the four bases. Helmets are mandatory.

Procedure: The pitcher has two options: Throw over to first base, or simulate a throw to the plate. You, the runner, are in a steal situation, watching the pitcher, and reacting accordingly. If the pitcher throws to the plate, you attempt to steal. If the pitcher throws over to first, you dive back properly. At each base, you have a different pitcher to read and react to.

Coach's Note: Remind the pitchers to perform with game-like intensity.

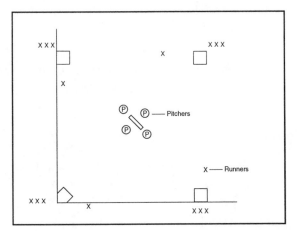 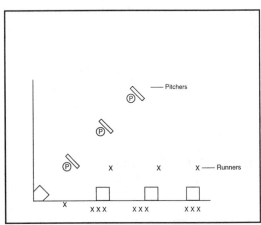

Two formats for the Baserunning Circuit I.

Variation: Instead of using the diamond as is, you may use throw-down rubbers and bases and set up additional stations along the first baseline.

#4 — BASERUNNING CIRCUIT II

Objective: To practice different baserunning situations.

Setup: A pitcher is on the mound and will throw from the stretch position. A catcher is at home plate in full gear. Runners are situated at each base.

Procedure: After taking a dry swing, runners at home will work on running from home, around first base. Runners at first will take a primary lead, a secondary lead, and react to a simulated ground ball. The runners at second will steal third. The runners at third will take their secondary lead and then tag up on a simulated fly ball. As the pitcher delivers the ball, a runner at each station will react to the situation. Thus, four players will run at once.

Coach's Note: Maintain full-speed intensity. Stress the importance of aggressive turns.

#5 — BASERUNNING CIRCUIT III

Objective: To practice different baserunning situations.

Setup: A pitcher is on the mound and will throw from the stretch position. A catcher is at home plate in full gear. Runners are situated at each base.

Procedure: The runners at home plate will simulate a suicide squeeze bunt and run from home to first base. The runners at first will attempt to steal. The runners at second will take a primary and secondary lead, and then attempt to score on a single. The runners at third will attempt to score on a squeeze bunt.

Coach's Note: Have a coach in the third base box who will direct the runner from second base to score on a single. Make sure the runners take their signal from the coach.

Variation: Remember, any baserunning situation can be implemented at one of the stations.

#6 — BASERUNNING CIRCUIT IV

Objective: To read pitches in the dirt.

Setup: A pitcher is on the mound and will throw from the stretch position. A catcher in full gear will receive the ball at home plate. Runners are positioned at first and second base only.

Procedure: The pitcher throws to the catcher. He deliberately throws many pitches in the dirt. The runners at both bases will take their primary and secondary leadoffs, read the pitch and react accordingly. If the ball is caught, runners will return to the base. If the ball is in the dirt, runners will react and take off for the next base immediately.

Coach's Note: If you can set up additional temporary bases a few feet behind the real bases, more players can participate on each pitch. For older age groups, the pitcher should use a variety of pitches so that the runners can learn to read breaking balls and change-ups.

Variation: If you don't wish to dedicate an entire circuit to anticipating balls in the dirt, include this drill as one station during the previously mentioned baserunning circuits.

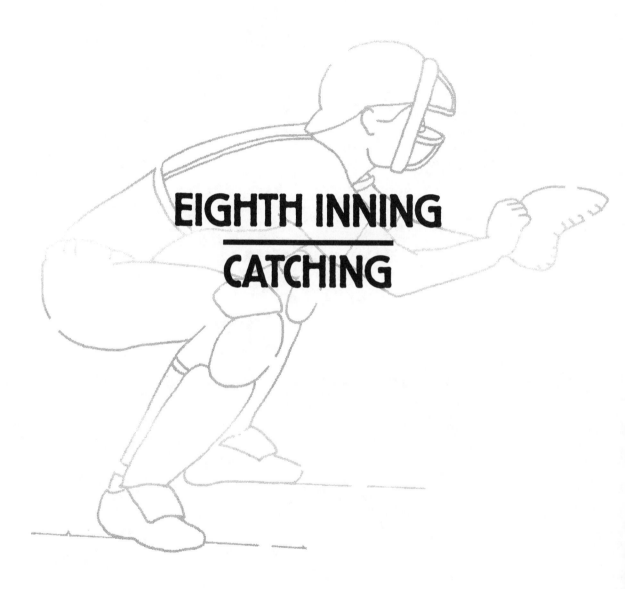

EIGHTH INNING
CATCHING

CATCHING: THE TOOLS OF IGNORANCE

The "tools of ignorance," a phrase frequently used in reference to catchers, pays less than due homage to these dedicated athletes. The catching position is easily the most underrated on a team. As a result, catchers are often neglected during instruction. And they usually get the fewest swings during batting practice.

While many coaches can recognize a good catcher, developing one is difficult. Clearly, they're a breed apart from the rest of their teammates. They work harder and are more active during a game than any other player on the team. They tend to play through more aggravating aches and pains than the rest of their teammates because toughness is expected of them. They're also easy targets for criticism. Catchers are a special case, so it's the responsibility of coaches to treat them accordingly. The days of treating catchers like homeless mongrels are gone. Instead, throw them a congratulatory bone once in awhile, and watch the results.

SETTING UP TO CATCH

Become familiar with two postures — the signaling position and receiving position. Be comfortable. It's no coincidence that catchers often develop bad knees which plague them in later life. They perform hundreds of knee bends almost daily, and that kind of abuse eventually takes its toll.

For the position used to provide signals to the pitcher, assume an athletic position with your body, feet, and shoulders facing the pitcher. From this pose, you can simply bend the knees into a crouch and rest on your haunches. Weight is evenly distributed on the balls of your feet with your heels off the ground. The toes will be slightly open, lined up with the baselines. Don't spread your feet too far apart, as this limits your mobility.

MAC FACT: *Open up the feet slightly so they are inside the baselines.*

Try to be comfortable in this position, since you'll be spending a lot of time in it. Keep your back straight and bend at the waist to achieve a slight forward angle. Feet are shoulder-width apart, with your head up.

When giving signals, your glove should be positioned outside and below the left knee, where it will conceal your intentions from the third base coach, who could relay the news to the hitter. Your throwing hand will give the signs deep in the groin area, back against the protective cup. Keep fingers deep but not so low that they dangle below the legs. Use the protective cup as the checkpoint for where you want to give your signals.

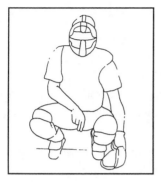

Signal-giving position.

Receiving position.

MAC FACT: *Hide your signs deep in the crotch area to keep the opposition from stealing the pitch selection.*

As a coach, create a uniform system of signs so that every player is in the know. Use the same signs, regardless of who's pitching. Doing so will avoid overall confusion.

After delivering the signals, shift into the receiving position. Your throwing hand should move behind your back, where it is protected from foul tips off the bat. A ball fouled off the bare hand can prove dangerous to you, and limit your ability to throw.

Position your glove in the middle of your body with your elbow out in front of your knees. It should be bent to allow for cushioning when the ball is received. Your hand is situated with the thumb pointing towards 3 o'clock, your glove establishing a clear target for the pitcher. Show the pitcher the target before he starts his delivery. This gives him time to take aim, which will help his control.

MAC FACT: *Give the pitcher a large target before he starts his delivery.*

Depending on the ability of the pitcher, set up so your glove is in the middle of your body, in the location where you want the ball to land. Move your whole body to establish location, not just the glove. This is the best position for a catcher receiving from an accurate pitcher. For less accurate pitchers, set up with your glove in the middle of home plate.

MAC FACT: *For accurate pitchers, set your target in mid-body, in the location where you want the ball to land. Set up in the middle of the plate only for inexperienced pitchers.*

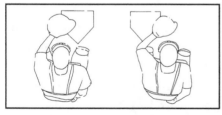

One of your knees should be directly in line with the middle of the plate so that the glove is located over either corner of the plate.

For experienced, accurate pitchers, move behind the plate and vary your location. One of your knees will often end up positioned in the middle of the plate on all pitches. Your other knee will be located either outside of home plate or on the inside of the plate (between the hitter and the plate), depending on the location that you called — inside or outside. From this setup position, your glove remains in the middle of your body, on the inside or outside part of the plate.

MAC FACT: *Position one knee in the middle of the plate, and the glove will be located in the middle of your body on the inner or outer half of home plate.*

RECEIVING THE BALL

Your prime job is to catch the ball; hitting and throwing are secondary. Over the course of the game, you'll receive over one hundred pitches, either balls or strikes. Perhaps thirty of these pitches are border-line calls. Your ability to handle the ball effectively can influence the call on most border-line pitches. If these pitches occur on three- and two-counts, then your receiving abilities are translated directly into base runners.

If the ball arrives in the strike zone, your job is to hold it there for the umpire to see. Never receive a pitch and move your glove immediately out of the strike zone. Make that pitch look as attractive as possible; lay each one out on the plate like a perfect, three-course gourmet meal. Think of yourself as a master chef.

"Funnel the ball" into the strike zone. Here's how: Visualize a funnel and notice how the large outer area gradually decreases in size. As a catcher, attempt to bring the ball into a smaller area. Funnelling the baseball doesn't involve movement of the whole glove. The action is directed by your wrists. Wrists will soften and cushion the ball into the strike zone. Glove movement is minimal in comparison to the wrist motion.

While receiving, visualize the borders of the square strike zone. These borders are the target areas for your wrists and glove as they funnel the ball. As the ball is received, your glove and wrist soften, and cradle the ball to the edge of the funnel or strike zone. Your wrist will roll back to the strike zone. Again, don't move the entire glove. Umpires feel unkindly toward you when you move the glove to the middle of the plate to try and deceive them into believing it was good. Umpires aren't fooled, especially when a pitch that was 4 inches off the plate suddenly jerks to the middle. Now that you've tried to deceive him, the umpire might call the pitch a ball, even if it was bordering the strike zone.

MAC FACT: *Receive the ball with your glove and elbow in front of your knees to cradle the ball into the strike zone.*

MAC FACT: *Don't move the entire glove; roll the wrist to cushion and funnel the ball into the strike zone.*

If the pitch is clearly out of the strike zone, return it immediately to the pitcher. Receive pitches to your glove side (left) with your thumb up. For balls at the top of the zone, the middle finger should face the sky with thumb in the 2 o'clock position.

Funnel the ball into the strike zone.

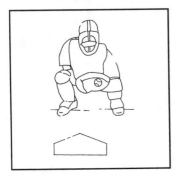

"Pick and stick" the low strike with
your fingers pointing up.

Pitches on the throwing side (your right) are more difficult to handle. Try to get your glove outside of the ball with the thumb pointed down. "Outside of the ball" means that if the glove remained there, the ball would pass between you and your glove. As you receive the ball, roll your wrist and funnel the glove back towards the corner of the plate. You're starting your glove out of the strike zone in an effort to funnel the ball back into the zone. Many catchers make the mistake of taking the glove to the ball, rather than cradling the ball back into the zone. The impact of the ball forces the glove further out and the ball appears to be out of the strike zone. By taking the glove outside of the zone first, momentum can assist your hand and wrist by coming back towards the strike zone.

MAC FACT: *To "funnel" properly, position your glove outside of the ball so you can come back towards the strike zone.*

If you have difficulty with pitches on the throwing side (your right), stagger that foot. Dropping the back foot slightly (3 to 5 inches, but no more) and opening it up might make it easier for glove movement across your body. Since it's harder to receive the ball across the body, this adjustment might make the difference.

Pitches in the lower part of the strike zone can be controversial. Some coaches believe that it's easier to turn your hand over so that your palm faces up, and catch the ball with the fingers pointing down. Professional catchers I've asked say that if they turn their hand over so the palm faces up, the umpire will automatically call it a ball. The biggest problem with catching low pitches with the fingers up is the tendency to take the glove lower and out of the strike zone when the ball hits your glove — "pick and stick" the baseball. In other words, pick the ball out of the air and stick it in the same spot to show the umpire that it is a strike. In order to do this, you must learn to receive the ball with a firm forearm but a loose wrist. The loose wrist will allow you to cushion and funnel even the low pitch back to the strike zone, while the firm forearm prevents the momentum of the ball from moving your glove down and out of the strike zone.

MAC FACT: *On low pitches, "pick and stick" the ball in the strike zone with your fingers still pointing up.*

Try to receive the ball as quietly as possible. Quiet receiving is not limited strictly to the ball and glove. This involves restricting the movement of the body and feet as well. Avoid quick and jerky actions behind the plate. Too much movement and wrestling around behind the plate becomes annoying to the umpire.

MAC FACT: *Limit your movement behind the plate so that you can receive the ball quietly.*

Develop and nurture a good relationship with your umpire. When questioning calls, do so with respect and you may be respected in return. Avoid turning around to the umpire to question calls, as it could be mistaken for showing him up. Keep your head facing the pitcher and engage in casual conversation. You can try comments and questions like: "Can you tell me where that pitch was, sir?"; "Was that a little too low?"; or "Geez, I really thought we should have got that call." Don't question the umpire on every pitch, of course. On the other hand, ongoing chatter over the course of the game shouldn't present problems. You may gain instant respect if you ask the umpire, during the pitcher's warm-up, where his zone is or where he likes the ball. Courtesy can only be beneficial to your team and pitcher at some point in the game.

MAC FACT: *Maintain a positive relationship with the umpire.*

Many players develop the habit of dropping or turning their glove after presenting the target, but prior to receiving the ball. Although it's okay to relax the tension in your arm and hand, be aware of letting the glove shift to a position which makes it difficult to catch the ball. Never catch the ball with the fingers pointing down. This automatically results in the umpire calling the pitch a ball. Also avoid pulling your glove back to your chest while waiting for the ball. In either case, your glove isn't in a good position to properly funnel the ball into the strike zone. Get the glove out in front and leave it there. With the exception of a slight relaxation of the hand, avoid too much glove movement.

BLOCKING BALLS IN THE DIRT

Your ability to block the ball can separate you from the rest of the pack. Together, receiving and blocking are the most important skills for catchers. My first summer coaching the Ontario provincial elite team featured some interesting personnel decisions at this key position. Ultimately, the catcher who earned the starting job was the one who was the least visible. The starting catcher stood out, not so much because of what he did, but for what the other catchers couldn't do. While others chased balls to the backstop or moved close pitches out of the strike zone, this young man quietly and confidently went about his job. This scenario really illustrated how the catching position is viewed. The positives are seldom recognized while mistakes are highlighted. One of the final catchers in camp was selected in the Major League Baseball draft that summer. Yet, despite demonstrating power as a hitter and a much stronger throwing arm than our number one catcher, our coaching staff placed a higher value on the receiving and blocking aspects of the game.

When a ball hits the dirt, keep it in front of you. This is accomplished by teaching the concept of "beating the ball to the ground." If the ball hits the dirt before you, the chances are you won't be quick enough to block it. However, if you beat the ball to the ground, then your chances of keeping it in front are greatly enhanced because your body is positioned properly as an obstruction for the ball to hit. Try to hit the dirt before the ball.

MAC FACT: *Keep the ball in front by "beating the ball to the ground."*

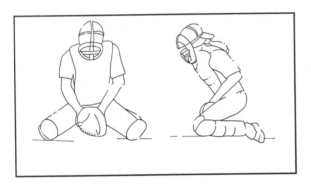

Create a good blocking position by forming a wall.

Blocking skills involve several movements. Drop to both knees immediately. Your glove will go straight down to the ground and fill the hole between your legs. Your bare hand will be placed behind your glove. You should now be in a position with no visible holes for the ball to scoot through. Keep your elbows at the side of your body in order to establish a wider base. Your chin should drop to the chest to protect your neck. Shape your body in a concave wall. Cup the ball with your body in order to keep it in front of you after it makes contact. This prevents your body from assuming a rounded position which would cause the ball to bounce off and away. Establish a broad base.

MAC FACT: *Form a concave wall with your body for the baseball to hit.*

Avoid popping up to get momentum toward the ground. Never lift your arms to get the body moving forward, as it takes you in a direction away from the objective of getting to the ground. It's a slower solution to a problem that demands quickness. Let the glove lead you to the ground. If the glove and fingers immediately turn over and drop forward to the ground, the rest of your body should follow.

Blocking a 100 mph missile with your body requires courage. Since protective gear isn't everything, the best thing you can do for yourself, having chosen this mission, is learn to do it right. Injuries often occur as a result of hesitation or fear. Stay relaxed. Let the ball hit you. Blocking is a passive activity once you get to the right location and assume the correct position. If you become active as the ball makes contact with your body, you risk both injury and the ball sneaking through a hole that might be created by a flinching movement. Being passive and letting the ball hit you will help soften the ball and reduce ricochet. Also, as you block a pitch, exhale. This release of breath eliminates tension in the muscles and deadens the ball closer to you.

MAC FACT: *Remain passive, and block. Let the baseball come to you.*

If the ball bounces away or over your body, it is not your fault. Get to the ground and smother any hops by creating a wall. Other than that, just hope that your pitcher gains some control!

Pitches that bounce in the dirt to your left or right require fast reaction skills. Establish an angle to cut the ball off. Push off your outside foot and slide on your shin guards to surround the ball. Not only must you beat the ball to the ground, you must also try to keep your shoulders square to the ball. Even if you are quick enough to achieve the blocking position before the pitch arrives, it may bounce off you to the side unless you can angle and square up your body to keep the ball in front.

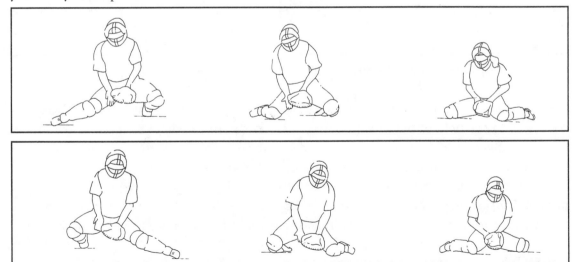

Push off the outside foot and slide on your shin guards to block balls left or right.

MAC FACT: *Push off the outside foot to block pitches which bounce left or right.*

Due to the velocity of a pitch, blocking baseballs is an extremely difficult task, demanding lots of repetitions and practice time. As a catcher you need to develop comfort and establish familiarity with the various skills required of you.

POP-UPS

A ball hit straight up in the air above home plate is an anxious moment for a catcher. Your greatest fear may involve your ability or inability to actually see the ball, so remove your mask and zero in without obstruction.

MAC FACT: *On pop-ups, get rid of your mask so you can zero in on the ball.*

On pop-ups, turn your back to the playing field and discard your mask once the ball reaches its peak.

Balls popped straight up have enormous backspin. To adjust to the rotation on the ball, turn your back to the field of play. As a general rule, most pop-ups will come back to the infield because of the spin. By turning your back to the field, you might locate the ball more easily and you've placed your body in the best position to adjust to the spin.

Wait for the ball to reach its height before discarding your mask. Throw your mask like you mean it, hard enough to hear it connect with the fencing of the backstop in a direction opposite to the ball. This way you know where it is and can avoid tripping on it as you pursue the ball.

MAC FACT: *Fire your mask against the backstop once the ball reaches its height.*

As usual, use two hands to make the catch. It's easy for balls to bounce out of your bulky catcher's mitt. Use your bare hand to wrap around the glove and keep the ball from popping out. Try to catch the ball above your head, making the play at or above eye level. This helps you see the ball into the glove and gives you some leeway to complete the catch if the ball pops out.

MAC FACT: *Catch all pop-ups with two hands above your head.*

Once the catch is made, turn immediately back to the infield to assess the baserunning situation. The runner may watch to see if you're paying attention, so react quickly and show that you're ready to throw them out if they get too aggressive on the base paths.

FIELDING BUNTS

Field bunts as any other player would, with an added responsibility for directing the play as it develops. You have a better view of the runners than the fielders who are running in with their back to the play. You must quickly decide who will field the ball and where it should be thrown.

Spring from your crouched position and straddle the ball as you approach it. The ball should be in the middle of your body and your feet should be lined up with the target. Your initial approach should establish the proper throwing direction. Set the feet first.

MAC FACT: *Set your feet in line with the target as you approach the ball.*

You should bend at the knees and scoop the ball with two hands into your belly button, your centre of gravity. Don't pick up the ball with only your bare hand, as this leads to an additional pat of the glove before throwing the ball. Scooping it with two hands ensures that you won't mishandle the ball when picking it up, and prevents glove patting.

Avoid fielding the ball too close to one of your feet. If the ball is mishandled, you'll be too far away to recover in time to complete the out. Field it in the centre of your body.

The location of the bunt will influence your approach to the ball. If the bunt is pushed up the first baseline, clear the runner's path. This means you will have a direct throwing lane to the first baseman. You want to avoid hitting the runner in the back with the ball. Take a power step away from the baseline once you scoop up the ball. A power step involves pushing away from the baseline with a powerful thrust. Your body should now be positioned several feet from the baseline. This power step should give you a direct route to throw the ball to the first baseman.

MAC FACT: *On bunts down the first baseline, take a power step away from the line to establish a direct throwing route.*

On bunts covering the area between the third baseline and the left side of the mound, take a direct route to the ball. As you approach the bunt, take a glove-side turn in order to set your feet in the direction of first base. A glove-side turn involves shifting the body so that you turn your back to the field. In doing so, step over and straddle the ball to set your feet.

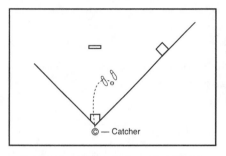

The banana curl: Your feet must immediately establish direction with your intended target.

Straddle the ball and scoop it up with two hands.

On bunts in the area between first base and the pitcher's mound, take a banana turn en route to the baseball. Similar to the route taken by the outfielders and base runners, you will curl before the ball so that you can approach the bunt with your feet already in the direction of first base. If you run straight to the ball, you'll lose time because you must set your feet to throw. Use your route to the ball to establish direction.

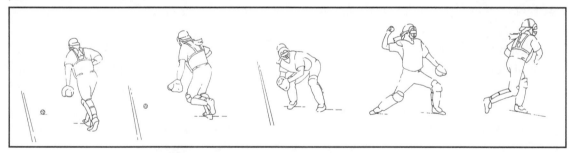

On bunts down the third baseline, take a glove-side turn to get the correct throwing position.

Once you've fielded the ball, you should have established good direction. If time permits, take a positive step towards the target by crossing your back foot in front and stepping to throw. If the play appears to be borderline, throw from the fielding position without taking the additional step.

Finally, whenever fielding a bunt, leave your mask on, since removing your mask is a time-consuming effort in a game decided by fractions of a second. Make sure your mask is tight enough so that it doesn't shift, but allows you to make the play.

THROWING OUT RUNNERS

If a runner is on base, make sure you're in position to react quickly enough to make a throw to second base. Both feet should be flat on the ground, weight distributed on the balls of your feet. Your thighs are parallel with the ground.

You want a quick release, so your throwing arm can't be behind your back. Make a fist and touch the back of your glove near the pocket. Your hand must be close enough to the glove to start the throwing process, yet not vulnerable to injury.

Receiving position with runners on base; your butt is low and thighs parallel to the ground.

MAC FACT: *When there are runners on base, the throwing hand will form a fist and hide behind the pocket of the glove.*

Young catchers need to be careful that in trying to establish a better pre-throwing position, they don't stand up. Even though thighs are parallel to the ground, keep your butt down. Angle your back at about a 45 degree angle to remain in a crouched position. The angle generated by your back also enables you to get your hands out in front of the knees to receive the ball.

As the pitch nears the hitting zone, start the throwing movements. Don't wait for the ball to be caught before initiating the throwing process. Get a head start. As with most baseball skills, the lower body plays a dominant role in throwing out runners. For this reason, you must learn the proper footwork

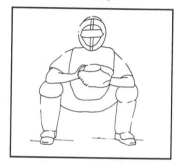

Front view of the receiving position with a runner on base. Your elbows and glove are in front of your knees.

first. Throwing footwork for the catcher is referred to as a "jump shift." A jump shift requires that you take a positive step towards second base and square the back foot. With this movement, both feet move to their respective spots quickly and simultaneously.

The release time is dictated by the quickness of your feet. For a quicker release, develop quicker feet. The jump shift is an explosive movement. The jump positions the feet, while the shift gets your shoulders in line to throw to the target. Together they generate power and momentum to deliver the baseball. The entire throwing process is similar to an airplane takeoff. Start low to the ground. Once you receive the necessary commands, explode out and then rise in a gradual progression. You shouldn't reach full height until after you've thrown. It is a rising action at a graduated slope. Upon releasing the baseball, you have moved forward. The proper footwork will place you closer to the target.

Use quick feet and rise gradually to throw.

MAC FACT: *Take an explosive positive step to second base while rising gradually.*

Your feet establish direction towards your target. Take the ball straight to your ear.

As you explode from your crouched position, keep your rear-end between the ball and the ground. Keeping your butt down prevents you from standing up to throw and puts you in a better receiving position. The transition from receiver to thrower must be quick.

Your upper body is important to the transition phase. Your throwing hand, previously located behind the pocket of your glove, will come around and turn the glove to place your hands palm to palm. Your glove hand will drive the ball into your bare hand all the way to your release point at the right ear.

Arm action also contributes to quicker release. Form a short arm circle and take the ball from the glove, straight to the ear, and throw. Your throwing elbow is still high, but the arc has been eliminated. It almost appears as if you short-arm the ball.

MAC FACT: *Catchers have no arc when throwing; the arm route is straight back to the right ear.*

Good catching techniques are:
- keeping your signs hidden from the opposing team
- establishing a visible target for the pitcher
- funnelling the ball to the strike zone
- receiving the ball quietly without distracting the umpire
- forming a wall at the plate to keep every pitch in front of you
- fielding all pop-ups above eye level with two hands
- when fielding bunts, setting your feet to throw and scooping the ball with two hands
- using an explosive jump shift to throw out potential base stealers

CATCHING DRILLS

#1 – RECEIVING DRILL I

Objective: To develop better receiving skills.
To funnel the ball into the strike zone.

Setup: Wear full catching equipment. A coach will stand sideways in front of you, about six feet away, with several baseballs.

Procedure: Coach snaps baseballs at the catcher in the same manner as the backhand flip by a middle infielder. She takes the ball across her body and then snaps it to the catcher so that she finishes like a traffic cop stopping a car. Tosses should be directed to various parts of the strike zone — high, low, inside and outside.

Receiving Drill I

Coach's Note: Catcher brings the ball back to the edge of the strike zone, with a slight wrist turn. The short distance will enable the ball to reach the catcher quickly enough to hone reflexes.

#2 – RECEIVING DRILL II

Objective: To practice the skill of funnelling.

Setup: Two catchers in full gear are in their crouch or receiving position about 10 feet apart. One baseball is needed.

Procedure: From the crouch position, snap a throw to your partner. Your partner will attempt to funnel the baseball into the strike zone. For a strike, she holds it there for the umpire to see. Then she will snap a throw back to you, and you perform the same drill.

Coach's Note: If the pitch is a ball, make certain it's returned to the other catcher, without funnelling. Stress the importance of good posture and encourage breaks every few throws to stretch the legs. Throws must be firm and accurate, as if in a real game.

Variation: Closer throws will result in greater accuracy and velocity, allowing the catcher to focus on the different parts of the strike zone.

#3 — POP-UP DRILL

Objective: To practice fielding pop-up balls around home plate.

Setup: As a coach, you will need a tennis racquet and a few tennis balls. Each catcher will be in full gear.

Procedure: Get into your crouch position at home plate. The coach will hit a tennis ball straight up in the air. He will decide when to yell "Go" to signal to the catcher that the ball is up. You will attempt to locate the ball, discard your mask, and then field the pop-up at or above eye level.

Coach's Note: Because the tennis ball is bouncy, the catcher is forced to use two hands to safely make the catch. The tennis racquet makes it easy to place the ball where you wish.

Variation: With older, more experienced players, add a second ball to the drill. Once the ball reaches its height, catapult another ball and have the catcher attempt to catch both of them. This makes the drill more difficult and challenging.

#4 — BUNT DRILL

Objective: To practice fielding bunts.

Setup: As catcher, you're positioned at home plate in full equipment. A coach or another catcher will stand behind you with baseballs.

Procedure: Start in your receiving position as if there was a runner on base. The coach or other catcher will toss out a "bunt" to various spots on the infield. You will spring forward and set your feet to field the bunt properly and make the throw. After three or four bunts, switch with your partner. Bunts should be tossed in various directions to work on different approaches.

Coach's Note: Concentrate on the footwork involved with fielding bunts correctly. Catchers should be working on developing quick feet. Make sure they keep their masks on while making the throw.

Variation: It's not essential to include a throw if that part of the field is not available. However, if the catchers are not going to throw the ball, at least have them simulate the throwing process.

#5 — WALL DRILL

Objective: To develop comfort when being hit by a ball thrown into the dirt.

Setup: As catcher, you are located at home plate with full gear on. The coach will stand about six feet away with several soft touch baseballs or other soft balls.

Procedure: Start on your knees in the blocking position with your glove and hand placed accordingly. The coach will throw five to eight balls consecutively. The throws will bounce in the dirt directly in front of you so that they bounce and hit you. Relax, and become familiar with being struck by a ball hit into the dirt. Breathe out as you are hit by the ball.

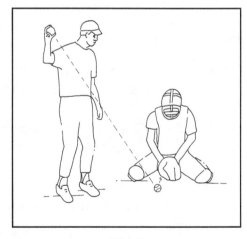

Wall Drill

Coach's Note: The use of the softer balls takes the fear factor out of skill development. Emphasize that the catchers are acting as walls, and that nothing should get through them. Watch for and eliminate any body tension in players.

Variation: Additional padding may be used to protect the exposed part of the bare arm, especially if the catchers are feeling beat up at the time.

#6 — HALF DISTANCE BLOCKING DRILL

Objective: To beat the baseball to the ground.

Setup: As catcher, start in receiving position at home plate. The coach will stand 20 to 30 feet away with a bucket of baseballs. The distance is relative to the age group.

Procedure: The coach will go through a pitching delivery and deliberately throw the ball into the dirt. You will drop to your knees as soon as you recognize the pitch is dirt-bound. After five to eight throws, switch with partner.

Coach's Note: Stress to catchers to "beat the ball to the ground." The catcher should drop to his knees and be a wall through which no pitch will pass. Throw an occasional strike to keep the catchers honest and prevent cheating and dropping to their knees too early.

Variation: You can use soft balls or real baseballs for this drill. Be sure to vary your pitches to get different hops on different sides of the plate.

#7 — DROP AND REACT DRILL

Objective: To develop blocking skills.
            To react to a blocked pitch when runners are on base.

Setup: Set up at home plate in full gear in the receiving position with runners on base. The coach will stand 20 to 30 feet from home plate.

Procedure: The coach will throw a pitch in the dirt. You will drop to your knees to block the pitch, then quickly scramble to your feet to react to the ball. Scoop up the ball with two hands, as you would when fielding a bunt.

Coach's Note: The goal of this drill is speed. Good base runners don't need the ball to bounce far in order to advance. A quick catcher can halt an opponent's running game.

Variation: Use soft or real baseballs. Have the catcher throw to a base, or simply go through the throwing process without releasing the ball.

#8 — UPPER BODY THROWING DRILL

Objective: To practice driving the glove and ball back to the ear during the transition. To reinforce the correct arm action of a catcher.

Setup: Partner up and stand 40 to 70 feet apart, one baseball between you.

Procedure: With toes pointing straight ahead, face one another. Throw the ball to your partner without moving your feet. Just rotate the upper body so that your shoulders line up with the target, and throw. Your partner will catch the ball with two hands and, using the glove, will drive the ball into the bare hand, back and up to the right ear. The glove should push back in a direct route with no arm circle. He will continue this action by throwing the ball back to you.

Coach's Note: Use this drill regularly, for short, intense periods.

Upper Body Throwing Drill

#9 — THROWING FOOTWORK DRILL

Objective: To develop the correct footwork for throwing to second base.

Setup: This drill can be performed anywhere. The only equipment needed is a baseball. The catcher can work with a coach or another catcher.

Procedure: Begin in the proper receiving position with runners on base. The coach or other player will throw a pitch of any distance, from a full 60 feet to just 7 feet. You will catch the ball and use a jump shift to get into throwing position. A positive step is required to start the throwing process. Take the correct arm route for a catcher and then simulate a throw.

Coach's Note: The focus of this drill is the footwork, not the end result. Make sure your throws focus the catcher on her feet, rather than her hands. Make sure she's low when exploding from the crouch. Strive for a quick release.

Variation: If you want the catcher to make a genuine throw, instead of a simulated toss, have the pitcher stand with his back to a screen or fence while the catcher throws into it. Throwing into the screen is beneficial because the catcher gets to finish the move without shifting his focus to the location of his toss. He is still concentrating solely on the mechanics of the throw.

#10 – FULL DISTANCE THROWING DRILL

Objective: To practice throwing out potential base stealers during game-like situations.

Setup: Assume your catching position at home plate in full gear. Your partner, or coach, will be at or in front of the pitcher's mound. A middle infielder is placed at second base to receive the throws.

Procedure: You will begin in correct receiving position with runners on base. Catch the pitch and make a strong, quick throw to second base using the jump shift footwork. Each catcher should take three to six repetitions and then switch up.

Coach's Note: Monitor the drill for correct throwing mechanics, and pay attention to players' footwork. Encourage the middle infielder to move to the base as the play develops. The drill should be performed in game-like conditions to accustom the catcher to throwing to the empty base, not the player. Have a hitter stand in the batter's box and swing over the pitch. The swing will prevent the catcher from cheating and springing forward too soon. Also, the swing will help the catcher become familiar with receiving the ball during real, live game distractions.

Variation: If a middle infielder isn't available, put a screen or garbage bucket at second base to serve as a target. However, whenever possible, place a middle infielder in position since this is an excellent drill for them as well.

NINTH INNING

THE WELL-ROUNDED PLAYER

THE WELL-ROUNDED PLAYER

In order to play baseball it is necessary to cultivate a variety of skills, and this necessity has led to a distinct specialization amongst players. At higher levels, players will rarely move to a different defensive position over the course of a season, let alone a single game. In fact, some players are so specialized that they do not play a defensive position at all. The Designated Hitter's sole asset to his team is his ability to swing the bat. He does not even attempt to hone his fielding skills.

This book espouses a different philosophy and approach. It is committed to the idea that players who are adept at fielding more than one position are of value to their teams at all ages and skill levels. These "utility" players can earn a spot on many teams simply because of their versatility. Coaches yearn for a player who can fill the void if they decide to pinch-hit for a weak player in the late innings. Since roster size is limited, the coach needs at least one player who is effective in many defensive positions.

Fortunately, most younger athletes have the privilege of experimenting with different positons. Indeed, the Little League coach who gives his players set positions is seriously cheating his athletes. No coach can be certain about the position a ten-year-old athlete should play. It is unfair for athletes who are still learning baseball skills to be restricted to the infield or outfield. The primary goal of a youth coach is simple: to develop the skills of each player on the team. In order to do so, he or she must teach athletes to improve their abilities in all areas. As each player advances in age and skill, it will become apparent which position should be his or her primary one. In some famous cases, players have changed position in the middle of their professional careers. Babe Ruth, one of the greatest hitters of all time, broke into the big leagues as a pitcher. Dave Steib, the first Toronto Blue Jay to throw a no-hitter, began his minor league career as an outfielder. Examples such as these illustrate why there is no need for the coach of eleven-year-olds to be overly concerned with assigning permanent positions to players. Instead, it is important to improve throwing arms, receiving skills and footwork.

Coaches can enhance the development of players in several ways. First, they should make an honest effort to offer solid and practical technical knowledge. They should also encourage questions and search for the answers. There is nothing wrong with a coach admitting that he or she does not have the answer to a player's question. Coaches can earn respect by seeking out the person who does possess the appropriate knowledge.

Second, coaches should establish solid practice plans that allow adequate time for skill development. Many coaches are so caught up with the idea of winning that they do not devote enough time to basic skill development. While first and third defences and bunt coverages are a part of the game, it is more valuable for beginning players to build arm strength and improve swing mechanics. A substantial component of any practice should include drill work and repetitions that improve fundamentals such as bunting, baserunning, throwing and receiving.

Third, coaches should remember that every athlete on the team deserves attention. Many coaches spend considerable time working with the weaker players in order to bring their skills up to par with those of the rest of the club. This attempt is admirable, but a little unfair to the better players. It is important not to ignore the more accomplished players. The top players may want and need extra help in order to improve, and the best player on a team may have a personal goal, such as becoming the best in the league or the region. A good coach should help him or her to achieve that objective. Other coaches may tend to focus solely on the top players and leave the weaker ones to fend for themselves. This approach is equally flawed. A coach cannot expect improvement if the players are not provided with the knowledge and opportunity to learn and develop.

Finally, a good coach should use his or her experience to teach life skills. Baseball is a game, and it is important to remember that once the game is over, life goes on. The positive impact of good coaches is often remembered years later. Every coach has values which can be conveyed to his or her players. For example, if punctuality is important to a coach, then he or she should make it an important component of the team's training program. Likewise, if a coach values camaraderie, then he or she should stress the importance of communication skills on the field and in life. While the playing field should not be a forum for political or religious beliefs, it may be the most structured and disciplined environment with which many young athletes come into contact. Good coaches can have an impact on the character as well as the physical development of their players.

The player, too, must take an active role in his or her development. Asking questions, listening and working hard are the keys to improvement. A player should realize that there is nothing wrong with asking a coach, "Why?" And coaches should be able to provide sound reasons for why they teach skills in a particular way. These reasons can motivate players to work hard at improving skills. Asking questions should not be confused with challenging the coach. Confrontations are not beneficial for anyone, player or coach. Asking a question in a polite and serious manner, however, should warrant a thoughtful response.

Players should also listen to their coaches. Often, players feel that they already know everything about the game. It is important not to fall into this trap. Coaches offer instruction because they sincerely wish to help players and build a good team. Players should remember that hard work is the key to improvement and success. Ability will only take them so far; there will always be someone better. Hard work is what bridges the gap between a player's potential and his or her actual performance. There is no magic formula for hard work — we all have the ability to improve. The willingness to unleash this ability is the key to success.

Good luck and have fun!

RECOMMENDED READING

Adair, Robert K. *The Physics of Baseball*. New York: Harper & Row Publishers, 1990.

Baker, Dusty, J. Mercer and M. Bittinger. *You Can Teach Hitting*. Indianapolis: Carmel, IN and Masters Press, 1993.

Bethel, Dell. *Coaching Winning Baseball*. Chicago: Contemporary Books, 1979.

Carew, Rod, A. Keteyian and F. Pace. *Rod Carew's Art and Science of Hitting*. New York: Viking Penguin, 1986.

Cluck, Bob. *Play Better Baseball*. Chicago: Contemporary Books, 1976.

Demonico, Rod. *Hit and Run Baseball*. Champaign: Leisure Press, 1992.

Delmonico, Rod. *Offensive Baseball Drills*. Champaign: Human Kinetics, 1996.

House, Tom. *The Pitching Edge*. Champaign: Human Kinetics, 1994.

Lopez, Andy and J. Kirkgard. *Coaching Baseball Successfully*. Champaign: Human Kinetics, 1996.

Polk, Ron. *Baseball Playbook*. Mississippi: Mississippi State, 1996.

Rose, Pete, and B. Hertzel. *Pete Rose's Winning Baseball*. Chicago: Contemporary Books, 1976.

Ryan, Nolan, and T. House. *Nolan Ryan's Pitcher's Bible*. New York: Simon & Schuster/ Fireside, 1991.

Seaver, Tom, and L. Lowenfish. *The Art of Pitching*. New York: William Morrow and Co., 1984.

Schmidt, Mike, and R. Ellis. *The Mike Schmidt Study*. Atlanta: McGriff and Bell, 1994.

Stockton, Bragg A. *Coaching Baseball: Skills & Drills*. Champaign: Human Kinetics, 1984.

Winkin, John, M. Coutts and J. Kemble. *Maximizing Baseball Practice*. Champaign: Human Kinetics, 1995.

FURTHER RESOURCES

Major Baseball Organizations – Canada

National Organization:

Baseball Canada
1600 James Naismith Drive, Suite 208
Gloucester, Ontario
Canada   K1B 5N4
Tel: 613 748-5606 / Fax: 613 748-5767
e-mail: baseball @rtm.cdnsport.ca
website: www.cdnsport.ca/baseball

Provincial Organizations:

Baseball Alberta
11759 Groat Road
Edmonton, Alberta
Canada   T5M 3K6
Tel: 403 453-8601 / Fax: 604 453-8603

Baseball British Columbia
200-1367 West Broadway
Vancouver, British Columbia
Canada   V6H 4A9
Tel: 604 737-3031 / Fax: 604 737-6043

Baseball New Brunswick
14 Lloyd Street
Hanwell, New Brunswick
Canada   E3C 1M4
Tel: 506 450-1891 / Fax: 506 444-9889

Baseball Nova Scotia
P.O. Box 3010, South Street
Halifax, Nova Scotia
Canada   B3J 1G6
Tel: 902 425-5450 / Fax: 902 425-5606

Baseball Ontario
16-1425 Bishop Street
Cambridge, Ontario
Canada   N1R 6J9
Tel: 519 740-3900 / Fax: 519 740-6311

Baseball Quebec
4545 Pierre de Coubertin
Montreal, Quebec
Canada   H1V 3R2
Tel: 514 252-3075 / Fax: 514 252-3134

Baseball Yukon
c/o Sport Yukon
4061 4th Avenue
Whitehorse, Yukon
Canada   Y1A 1H1
Tel: 867 633-6968 / Fax: 867 633-4715

Manitoba Baseball Association
200 Main Street
Winnipeg, Manitoba
Canada   R3C 4M2
Tel: 204 925-5763 / Fax: 204 925-5792

Newfoundland Amateur Baseball Association
83 Ashford Drive
Mount Pearl, Newfoundland
Canada   A1N 3N7
Tel: 709 368-2819 / Fax: 709 368-6080

Prince Edward Island Amateur Baseball Association
P.O. Box 92
Morell, Prince Edward Island
Canada   C0A 1S0
Tel: 902 961-2420 / Fax: 902 961-7339

Saskatchewan Baseball Association
1870 Lorne Street
Regina, Saskatchewan
Canada   S4P 2L7
Tel: 306 780-9237 / Fax: 306 352-3669

Major Baseball Organizations — United States

National Organizations:

American Baseball Coaches Association
108 South University Avenue, Suite 3
Mount Pleasant, Michigan
USA   48858-2327
Tel: 517 775-3300 / Fax: 517 775-3600

USA Baseball Association
3400 East Camino Campestre
Tucson, Arizona
USA   85716
Tel: 520 327-9700 / Fax: 520 327-9221
website: www.usabaseball.com/

NOTES

NOTES

NOTES

NOTES

BRIGHT LIGHTS FROM POLESTAR

Polestar Book Publishers takes pride in creating books that enrich our understanding of the world and ntroduce discriminating readers to exciting writers. These independant voices illuminate our history, stretch the imagination and engage our sympathies. Here are some of our best-selling sports titles.

Behind the Mask: The Ian Young Goaltending Method, Book One
Ian Young and Chris Gudgeon
Drills, practice techniques, equipment considerations and more are part of this unique goaltending guide.
$18.95 Can / $14.95 USA

Beyond the Mask: The Ian Young Goaltending Method, Book Two
Ian Young and Chris Gudgeon
Book Two of this effective goaltending series focuses on intermediate goalies and their coaches.
$18.95 Can / $14.95 USA

Celebrating Excellence: Canadian Women Athletes
Wendy Long
A collection of biographical essays and photos that showcases more than 200 athletes who have achieved excellence.
$29.95 Can / $24.95 USA

Get the Edge: Audrey Bakewell's Power Skating
Audrey Bakewell
Skating specialist Audrey Bakewell provides basic and advanced drills for power skating, a skill fundamental to the game of hockey.
$18.95 Can / $16.95 USA

Hockey's Young Superstars
Eric Dwyer
Profiles and action photos of Bure, Jagr, Lindros, Mogilny, Sakic, Modano and others.
$9.95 Can / $8.95 USA

Long Shot: Steve Nash's Journey to the NBA
Jeff Rud
Profile of young NBA star Steve Nash, detailing the determination and skill that carried him through high school and college basketball, and into the ranks of the pros.
$18.95 Can / $16.95 USA

Lords of the Rink
Ian Young and Terry Walker
Here is every goaltenders handbook, including physical and psychological techniques, and many game-action photos. The final book in the Ian Young goaltending trilogy.
$18.95 Can / $14.95 USA

Our Game: An All-Star Collection of Hockey Fiction
Doug Beardsley, editor
From the Forum to the backyard rink, this collection of 30 stories illuminates the essence of the hockey soul.
$18.95 Can / $16.95 USA

Thru the Smoky End Boards: Canadian Poetry About Sports and Games
Kevin Brooks and Sean Brooks, editors
The glory of sport is celebrated in this anthology of poems from more than 70 poets.
$16.95 Can / $14.95 USA

Too Many Men on the Ice: Women's Hockey in North America
Joanna Avery and Julie Stevens
A fascinating look at all levels of women's hockey in Canada and the United States, including in-depth profiles of prominent players.
$19.95 Can / $16.95 USA

Polestar titles are available from your local bookseller.
For a copy of our catalogue, contact:
Polestar Book Publishers, publicity office
103-1014 Homer Street
Vancouver, British Columbia
Canada V6B 2W9
polestar@direct.ca
http://mypage.direct.ca/p/polestar